Futures Unlimited:
Teaching About Worlds To Come

Robert M. Fitch and Cordell M. Svengalis

Center for Teaching Library
The Westminster Schools
1424 West Paces Ferry Road, N.W.
Atlanta, Georgia 30327

National Council for the Social Studies • Bulletin 59

NATIONAL COUNCIL FOR THE SOCIAL STUDIES

About the Authors

ROBERT M. FITCH is Professor of Social Studies and Education at the University of Iowa, Iowa City, Iowa. He has served as a member of the International Activities Committee of the National Council for the Social Studies, and is also a member of the World Future Society. Dr. Fitch has co-authored textbooks on secondary education and articles and reviews in such journals as *Social Education*, *The Social Studies,* and *Human Organization*. He presently teaches social studies methods and curriculum courses as well as a course entitled "Futurism in Education."

CORDELL M. SVENGALIS received a Ph.D. in Social Studies Education from the University of Iowa. He has been a junior high and high school social studies teacher, and an Assistant Professor of Education at Cornell College, Mount Vernon, Iowa. He has contributed articles and reviews to *Education Tomorrow* and *The Social Studies*. Dr. Svengalis is a member of the World Future Society, the National Council for the Social Studies, and Phi Delta Kappa. He is presently Director of Admissions for the Graduate Program in Urban and Regional Planning at the University of Iowa.

Library of Congress Catalog Number: 79-52124
ISBN 0-87986-023-5
Copyright © 1979 by the
NATIONAL COUNCIL FOR THE SOCIAL STUDIES
2030 M Street, N.W. Washington, D.C. 20036

Foreword

As I read the galleys for this Bulletin, my reactions were as much emotional as they were intellectual. The emotions triggered were, in equal parts, pride, envy, and gratitude. As a candidate for the NCSS Board of Directors in 1971, I had written, "We must also look beyond current problems. Changes wrought by science and technology have outpaced the capacity of our social institutions. Nuclear power, computer technology, environmental crises, and population problems regularly are discussed in classrooms. Recent developments in biology in general and genetics in particular are truly revolutionary and are generating significant social problems. NCSS should promote the development of approaches that bring relevant elements of the social sciences, the humanities, and the natural sciences together for effective social studies education." I was proud that NCSS was publishing a Bulletin that spoke directly to my concerns and envious that I had not written it.

As a classroom teacher I am most grateful to the authors for providing practical examples of teaching strategies and lists of recommended resources for teachers and students. Ever since Daniel Roselle introduced me to the uses of science fiction with the February, 1973, issue of *Social Education* on "Teaching World History Through Science Fiction," I have been a "Futures" teacher. This Bulletin addresses my need for material on the "what" and "how" of futures education. Chapter 3, "Innovative Methods for Teaching About the Future"; Chapter 5, "Images of the Future Through Science Fiction";

and Chapter 7, "Resources for Teaching About the Future" will be the most frequently used sections of my copy of the Bulletin.

The "why" of futures education also receives careful attention in this Bulletin. The futures field is surveyed and placed in historical perspective. Several curriculum approaches to teaching about the future are presented. The values dimension of futures education is thoroughly discussed, and useful suggestions are made about evaluation of the outcomes of futures education.

In Chapter 1, as a part of their theoretical discussion of the futures field, the authors state: "Futurism is concerned with predictions and forecasts about the future. But, more importantly, futurism is concerned with helping individuals develop understandings, attitudes, and abilities which in turn help them deal more effectively with change and with the social responsibilities of living in a technological society." They contend that futures education should be about change, choices, decisions, and consequences. But choosing not to change remains an alternative in any specific situation. Neither the present nor the past is rejected.

A few months ago I shared an unexpected and satisfying experience. At a gathering of my former college classmates, our freshman English teacher read us excerpts from papers we had written for him in 1951. Each of us had written a description of the grandparent whom he or she most admired. The original purpose of the assignment had been to provide material for writing a history of our grandparents' era from our collective frame of reference. What came through most strongly some 28 years later was our common appreciation of hard work, triumph over adversity, concern for others, and personal integrity. These were the standards by which we measured others then. They remain as standards by which we judge ourselves today. That experience provided great comfort to me as a teacher and as a parent concerned about the ability of the young to cope with change.

Continuity and change can coexist, and this Bulletin provides further support for those who hope that condition can be maintained.

Robert M. Fitch and Cordell M. Svengalis are optimistic about the future and about the capacities of the young. That optimism permeates this Bulletin. NCSS is privileged to publish their work, and I am honored to thank them officially for their contribution to the organization and to social studies education.

George G. Watson, Jr., *President*
National Council for the Social Studies

Preface

The desire of increasing numbers of teachers to include some form of instruction about the future is being manifested in a wide variety of ways in classrooms across the country. Such diversity represents teacher effort and creativity at their best, since as yet there are few guidelines for educational programs reflecting the futures perspective.

This Bulletin represents our analysis of this innovative idea. We have attempted to provide both a theoretical framework and a number of practical suggestions for individuals who wish to explore some of the many possibilities for teaching about the future. Futures education, we believe, contains some exciting possibilities for enriching the social studies curriculum. As with any innovation, however, there are also a number of controversies and potential misapplications.

It is our hope that this Bulletin will contribute to an understanding and acceptance of the futures education perspective, and will help to stimulate further efforts to deal with the unresolved issues.

Robert M. Fitch and Cordell M. Svengalis
University of Iowa

Illustration Credits

Page VIII. Astronaut L. Gordon Cooper, his silver suit flickering in the mid-Pacific sun, steps out of his spacecraft, "Faith 7," into the deck of the recovery ship after 22 orbits in space. Artist: Mitchell Jamieson. Source: National Aeronautics and Space Administration.

Page 20. The "Agrisphere," a 40-foot-high geodesic dome of aluminum and mirrored plexiglas, highlighted the International Harvester farm exhibit at Chicago's Museum of Science and Industry. Inside the dome, an 80-capacity theatre featured a 16-minute multimedia presentation on the past, present, and future of farming. Source: National Aeronautics and Space Administration.

Page 30. An artist's concept depicting the completed Solar Power Satellite in geosynchronous orbit some 36,000 miles above the Earth. The two antennas are transmitting microwave energy to the Earth below for conversion to conventional electrical power. Source: National Aeronautics and Space Administration.

Page 46. Artist Pierre Mion's painting of "Astronauts Explore the Moon." It dramatizes the immense size of the lunar craters and mountains on the lunar surface. Source: National Aeronautics and Space Administration.

Page 60. This artist's rendering of a view of the endcap and living quarters illustrates the variations in gravity in a space colony. Each cylinder rotates on its axis once every 114 seconds to create Earth-like gravity on the perimeter of the colony. As one moves toward the central axis, artificial gravity produced by the centrifugal force of the colony's rotation diminishes, until at the axis itself an individual would be weightless. Source: National Aeronautics and Space Administration.

Page 68. 21st-Century Space Colony. The reader must imagine himself or herself as a 21st-century resident of a space colony who is returning home after a holiday on Earth. The 32 kilometer (19 mile) long, 6400 meter (4 mile) diameter cylinder at the right and its twin at the left are seen as they would appear from an approaching spaceship some 32 kilometers (20 miles) away. Source: National Aeronautics and Space Administration.

Page 76. This painting, entitled "One Man's Lifetime," illustrates the progress made in the conquest of space in the span of one person's lifetime. The artwork is by Roland O. Powell, a senior illustrator with Kentron Hawaii, Ltd., a subsidiary of the LTV Corporation. Source: National Aeronautics and Space Administration.

Page 84. Photograph of an integrated circuit chip placed next to a dime. Single chips of this kind are presently used in calculators, microwave ovens, and many other products where "microprocessors" are utilized for control or computation. The chip is, in effect, a small computer, for it has the necessary logic circuits and memory circuits to perform computations. Source: Burroughs Corporation.

Acknowledgments

We wish to thank, first of all, the NCSS Publications Board for giving us the opportunity to prepare this Bulletin. We are also indebted to editor Daniel Roselle for contributing many valuable suggestions, and for his support and encouragement.

Many other individuals contributed directly and indirectly to our enlightenment concerning the subject. Without their pioneering work, this Bulletin would not have been possible. Errors of interpretation, of course, remain our responsibility.

Finally, we wish to express gratitude to our typist, Barb Recker, who performed service above and beyond the call of duty in typing and retyping earlier drafts and the final copy of the manuscript.

Contents

1.
The Futures Field: We Have Met the Future and It Is US

The Exploration and Discovery of the Brave New World of the Future

Exploration and discovery are historical concepts generally first encountered by students in their fifth-grade United States history textbook. The terms are used to describe that period in the past designated as the early Renaissance. Typically, such textbooks begin with a treatment of the antecedents of discovery and cite the intellectual ferment that resulted in the early voyages of exploration. The net effect of the narrative which follows is to create the impression that the events which transpired from then to the present were destined to occur. Thus, it might be said that today we are beginning a new phase of exploration and discovery.

Just as some individuals of the fifteenth century hypothesized that there was something "out there" to be explored and discovered, so individuals of the twentieth century are hypothesizing that there is something "out there" to be explored and discovered. For the person of the fifteenth century, "out there" was a route to the East, new lands, and trade and riches, with the potential for a better life. For the person of the twentieth century, "out there" is a temporal-mental exploration of alternative futures, with the potential for a better life. As with most historical analogies, this one has deficiencies. Perhaps the most serious one is that the future is not just "out there" to be discovered and explored, but it is *created* as a function of our present actions. Still the analogy is

useful in that it provides the justification for beginning our exploration of futures education by an examination of conditions antecedent to it.

The Discovery of the Future

Since World War II, and especially over the past decade, interest in and concern about the future have grown rapidly; and we are in the process of reconceptualizing our ideas of exploration, discovery, and the future.

Perhaps the greatest impetus to this reconceptualization has come from the gradual realization of increasingly serious crises facing the world. Among these crises are the threat of nuclear war, increasing problems of pollution, and growing population pressures on food supplies, living space, and other resources. With these problems has come the recognition of the finiteness of the earth's non-renewable resources, and growing pressures for the conservation and more equitable distribution and consumption of the world's resources.

Not only are many of these problems worldwide in their implications, but they have arisen in a comparatively short span of time. The so-called J-curve is a graphic representation of the rapidity with which various events, circumstances, and developments have taken a steeply ascending path. The combination of the total number of such J-curves gives us an in-

The real future is no mechanical continuation of the present, which can be projected by a simple curve on a graph. From moment to moment the inertia of the past may be altered by new factors springing from both inside and outside the human personality.

—Lewis Mumford

dication of the total rate of change in society. This accelerating rate of change is the subject of Alvin Toffler's *Future Shock,* which first appeared in 1970. As Toffler put it:

> Much that now strikes us as incomprehensible would be far less so if we took a fresh look at the racing rate of change that makes reality seem, sometimes, like a kaleidoscope run wild. For the acceleration of change does not merely buffet industries or nations. It is a concrete force that reaches deep into our personal lives, compels us to act out new roles, and confronts us with the danger of a new and powerfully upsetting psychological disease. This new disease can be called "future shock," and a knowledge of its sources and symptoms helps explain many things that otherwise defy rational analysis.[1]

Other observers, looking beyond the possibilities of catastrophe, believe that we are merely experiencing the growing pains of a transition to a higher level of civilization, and that we are living through a period of change comparable to the Agricultural or Industrial Revolutions. However, two facts stand out: Seldom in history have individuals been witness to changes of comparable velocity or pervasiveness occurring within the time span of a single generation; and never before have human activities had such global significance.

Time and Stereotypes

The future is an idea often referred to but seldom reflected upon. Perhaps one reason for this is that the only certainty of our knowledge about the future is death.

All else is uncertain (except perhaps change). Anxiety has been characterized by one psychologist as the gap between "now" (the present) and "then" (the future).[2] Not knowing what the future will bring produces an understandable aversion to reflection.

Yet the importance of developing some conception of the future has been noted by anthropologists and other scholars. That different cultures and sub-cultures perceive time differently has likewise been observed and contributes to the sterotyping of culture.[3] Thus, distorted stereotypes would have us believe Latins are relaxed, and will put off tasks until tomorrow. People of the United States, by contrast, are said to be impatient and always in a hurry to move into the future. Time, then, and our alleged and real attitudes toward it form a crucial dimension of futurism.

But time is basically an arbitrary and subjective concept. The future is complex and has meaning only as we supply other dimensions. In this chapter we will examine such dimensions. However, it will be useful to view first the historical development of futurism by examining some of the leading theorists and their ideas.

Futurism and the Development of Concern for the Future

Futurism is currently known by a confusing aggregate of names, among which are futuristics, futures studies, futures research, futurology, futuribles, and prognostics. Each term reflects the orientation, focus, and/or personal preference of the user. The term "futurism," which is our preference, is concerned with philosophy and style and, according to Edward Cornish, editor of *The Futurist,* "may . . . be used to designate an attitude or movement that emphasizes the future."[4] As individuals become more familiar with the study of the future, and as the field becomes more clearly established, other terms may be preferred.

To the general public, however, the field remains generally undifferentiated from a wide variety of unscientific practices which have been employed throughout history to foretell the future. Historically, attempts to see into the future have occupied a portion of human activity since the dawn of civilization. For the most part, however, they have focused on prophesying the occurrence of events over which individuals have little or no control. Even today, many predictive activities—such as weather forecasting and demographic projections—are attempts to provide information about specific events which may affect activities in which planning is important.

By contrast, contemporary futurism can be distinguished by a more active and systematic orientation toward a range of alternative future possibilities, rather than toward a single predicted future occurrence. This perspective has evolved from a long history of attempts to combine knowledge of the past, present, and future.

Some of the best examples of this tradition of suggesting alternative futures can be found in utopian and dystopian (anti-utopian) literature, which ranges from Plato's *Republic* to Ernest Callenbach's more recent *Ecotopia,* and which also includes the visions of other individuals throughout history. Sir Thomas More, Sir Francis Bacon, St. Augustine, Robert Owen, Samuel Butler, Edward Bellamy, H. G. Wells, Aldous Huxley, George Or-

well, and many others down through the ages have composed imaginative images of the future.[5] Although the subject matter varies widely, most of these are visions of future societies which their creators believed were possible.

The long history of utopian literature demonstrates that for over two thousand years individuals of vision have believed that the powers of human intelligence, free will, choice, and action can work together to influence the future. The realization of this fact is now enabling futurism to become an accepted and academically respectable perspective.

Selected Futurists and Their Ideas: European Origins and Approaches

A number of individuals in both Europe and the United States have made significant contributions to the development of futuristic theory and practice. The selection included here is primarily intended to represent the range and depth of the ideas which identify the futuristic perspective in its broadest sense.

The development of an academic and scientific approach to futurism can be traced to the work of four European scholars. Futurism in the United States has derived many of its theoretical foundations from them.

Ossip Flechtheim and Futurology

One of the early scholarly attempts to define and delineate the study of the future was made by Ossip Flechtheim, who coined the term "futurology" in the 1940s.[6] This activity, he suggested, might be considered either as a pure science, applied science, or something similar to a philosophy. Futurology included projections, predictions, and planning procedures, as well as goals, norms, and values concerning the future.[7] The function of futurology was to facilitate a radical-constructive "criticism of the status-quo" and to get societies to become more future-oriented. In addition, since the idea of the inevitability of world progress is so pervasive, the use of pessimistic or dystopian images of the future was necessary to the presentation of more balanced outlooks.[8]

Flechtheim cautioned that people will not necessarily continue to make progress, but that Western Civilization may decline and collapse, leading to the emergence of a new "dark age."[9] In order to prevent societies from moving blindly into an unknowable future, he believed that scholars and educators should use accumulated knowledge and wisdom to transform education in ways which would include the study of the future. Unlike courses such as history, government, economics, and sociology, which end with the present, they would go beyond, into the future. Such courses, which would include past, present and future, would become more complete and meaningful.[10]

Thus, futurology was not so much a new or special branch of knowledge, but was instead a new kind of synthesis of materials from a variety of sources. This was the transdisciplinary or integrating function of futurology, in which ideas and concepts from several disciplines were combined in ways which more closely reflected reality and which facilitated a better understanding of the present with all its complexities.[11]

Futurology was also closely related to history and could be characterized as a projection of history into a new time dimension.[12] Reflection upon Flechtheim's assertion suggests a number of strong similarities between the study of the past and the study of the future: Both involve the concept of chronology; both involve the study of societal issues, trends, and events, as well as their implications for subsequent events; both involve the use of data to make generalizations, speculations, and judgments; and both involve the use of imagination and interpretation to draw conclusions. One specific example of this relationship between futur-

ology and history is that both place considerable emphasis on patterns, cycles, and trends in order to understand possible cause and effect relationships.

Futurology was a useful beginning to developing a discipline of futurism. It was limited, however, to the task of forecasting the future so that the upper classes could protect themselves against "social tempests, cultural deluges and historical catastrophes"; and, in the event of a collapse of civilization, would enable those fortunate and foresighted individuals to preserve their culture, and presumably themselves.[13]

Bertrand de Jouvenel and Futuribles

Futurism took on a different perspective as a result of the reflections of the French scholar Bertrand de Jouvenel. He prefers the use of the term "futuribles" to designate those things which can be deduced by the mind from the present state of things, but which do not yet exist.[14]

De Jouvenel combines ideas about the future with concepts of human intelligence and the human will. He makes a crucial distinction between the past and the future: Facts, he asserts, belong to the realm of the past. We can know them, but have no power to change them. They can be verified as being true or false, but, since they represent something already accomplished, we have no power over them. We can know the past with a reasonable degree of certainty, even though historians do not always agree on causal factors and precise details; but we are not free to alter what has already happened. By contrast, the future is a field of uncertainty, but at the same time a field of liberty and power. The future is a field of likelihoods, possibilities, and probabilities.[15]

The future is the domain of the person of action, who uses his or her powers and abilities to increase the likelihood that his or her imagined future will occur.[16] Facts from the past—and this includes all facts, since they become part of the past as soon as they occur—are useful only as the raw material out of which the mind makes estimates of the future.

Representing the future in the mind, through foresight, is a natural and necessary human activity. In societies which tend to be routine, conservative, and relatively unchanging, knowledge of the future is fairly certain because the future will most likely resemble the past. Therefore, the activity of looking ahead to a radically different future, in such a traditional society, is relatively meaningless. In rapidly changing societies, however, where uncertainty is the rule rather than the exception, the development of anticipatory skills becomes much more important.[17] If we believe, as the evidence suggests, that Western Society is in fact undergoing unprecedented, increasingly accelerated change for which there are no reliable "guidebooks" or "roadmaps," we will have to become familiar with a wide variety of anticipatory "tools" if we are to direct ourselves intelligently in the coming decades.

A further aspect of futuribles suggests that by thinking about the future we can categorize our mental representations into: (1) those futures which are possible, (2) those futures which are probable, and (3) those futures which are desirable.[18] The major element in this idea is that "there are many future states of affairs which we have no reason to regard as impossible."[19] This represents the notion of *alternative* futures as opposed to the idea of a predetermined future which is beyond the power of human control.

The process of examining possible and probable futures in order to choose desirable ones can be regarded as the development to a higher plane of one of the major qualities which distinguish humankind from the rest of the animal kingdom; namely, the ability to anticipate and plan, to be "pro-active" rather than simply reactive.[20] Pro-active behavior is made possible by mental images, which are representations of reality past and present, and intellectual constructions of future possibilities. Human action is the result of exercising the will toward mental objects; e.g., goals. Individuals are motivated by such mental images and seek to validate appealing ones and avoid unappealing ones.

Thus, de Jouvenel appears as a strong advocate of conscious, purposeful, sustained, and systematic human action which will validate the notion of people as the creators of the future.

Fred Polak and Prognostics

Fred Polak is a Dutch scholar for whom the study of the future is an emerging scientific discipline which shows promise for moving humankind toward an increasingly managed future. He uses the term "prognostics" to indicate his approach to the study of the future. This term involves a set of mental attitudes, as well as a variety of both quantitative and qualitative techniques.

Extending some of the major ideas from de Jouvenel's futuribles, Polak states that in looking toward the future we must consider: (1) the various possibilities which lie before us, (2) the various possible developments which are also desirable, and (3) "those desirabilities which remain after a careful process of elimination and may also be considered as potentially realizable through the effective application of human power."[21]

Polak calls for a combination of quantitative and qualitative techniques in order to explore properly the desirabilities and realizabilities of imagined futures. The components of his qualitative thinking approach include: intuition ("to provide random access to all spheres and levels of human thought, or human sense and appreciation");[22] fantasy (to provide vision); creativity (to invent the future "by formulating dynamically compelling, idealistic visions of the future, by drawing up blueprints for the future, and by artistically creating logically consistent sketches of the future"); and brainstorming (a pooling of ideas from many individuals, which can be combined in various ways, amplified, and revised).[23] He also places considerable emphasis on the importance of a normative sense of purpose as being a vital ingredient in futures research and forecasting. In particular, the roles of values and goals must be openly acknowledged as indispensable to the proper examination of future alternatives.[24]

A scientific theory of the future, he asserts, must emerge from our ability to see a distinction between those things which are likely to occur without human intervention, and those desirabilities which will emerge only after purposive, scientifically-based action. Objectives, directions, directives, and standards are all necessary to move society steadily in the direction of desirable futures.[25]

The fact that societies do not appear to be moving in this direction indicates to Polak a missing variable. This he attempts to provide by applying his concept of "images of the future."

The future is born, he suggests, out of people's capacity to imagine a future. The increasing sophistication of people's time-consciousness enables them to push out the frontiers of the unknown. We must draw mental boundaries of the future, take account of the consequences of our actions, and increase our knowledge as we leave the familiar and venture into the unknown. It is by imagining and perceiving the future that we enable ourselves to shape the future.[26] Such images of other worlds and other times are major factors in propelling the forces of history. These images of the future might be thought of as tools to be used in shaping the actual future and are necessary, he claims, to social progress: "The rise and fall of images of the future precedes or accompanies the rise and fall of cultures. As long as society's image is positive and

flourishing the flower of culture is in full bloom. Once this image begins to decay and lose its vitality, however, the culture does not long survive."[27]

The term "images of the future" is used by Polak for "those condensed and crystallized expectations prevailing among peoples in certain periods and developed into systematic projections toward the future. They may be of a transcendental-religious character, pertaining mainly to the end of time or to last things (eschatological), or they may concern themselves mainly with social humanitarian ideals for the good society on earth (utopian)."[28] The role of such images has been of considerable importance throughout history. These images, designed by the elites of their respective societies, are passed on to the masses where they arouse passion and faith.

As things stand at the present time, Polak laments, Western culture is lacking in the kinds of good and desirable images which are necessary for the periodic renewal of society.[29]

Robert Jungk and Participatory Futurism

For Robert Jungk, founder of the European Mankind 2000 project and convener of the resulting futures conferences, the major task in preparing for the years ahead is to unleash the creative potential in "everyman" and to democratize the future. People do not, he suggests, have to be at the mercy of uncontrollable forces such as technology. Instead, they can control the ends toward which societies evolve through the thoughtful application of new ideas generated by study groups, committees, commissions, etc., in which as many people as possible are invited to become involved.[30]

Jungk's writings on the future can thus be distinguished from those of Flechtheim, de Jouvenel, and Polak (all of whom deal primarily with the theroretical features of the concept of a future-oriented philosophy) by his detailed and practical orientation toward "doing" the future. He approaches the future on two broad fronts: (1) the need for broad, democratic participation in the process of determining societal goals, and in such joint action as is necessary to achieve such goals, and (2) the need to transform educational systems and other institutions in ways which would make them more likely to produce individuals who are more imaginative and creative, and who will take more active roles in helping to achieve desirable futures.

Conservatism and hostility toward change, he suggests, are two of our most immediate human problems. For example, when existing structures, business profits, "national security," or other types of self interests are perceived as being threatened, resistance to change becomes particularly strong. Innovations, in particular, are often regarded by some as "dangerous, destructive and uncertain. They are enemies of orderly, planned activity. They turn everything upside down and do nothing but harm. By all means let us speak of innovations, let us study, praise and embrace them—only do not let us promote them."[31]

Contributing to this attitude of conservatism is a blindness about the future which is due, he says, not only to a lack of education about the future, but also to the narrow specializations in the various disciplines, which contribute to the failure of scholars to communicate with one another and to society as a whole. The role of information in helping to provide the basis for a better future is obvious; but a more crucial need is a greater effort to synthesize this information (which is readily available in discrete segments but inadequately combined into more meaningful wholes) by the use of computers, by establishing interdisciplinary "teams," and by the training of more "generalists."[32]

"The future," says Jungk, "begins in the schools."[33] He states that if the schools were transformed into institutions which encouraged more imaginative and creative thinking, other institutions might eventually be transformed as well. He praises examples of schools which "are no longer like factories for making citizen-subjects or obedient consumers."[34] They are, instead, "seed-beds of social change," which, though they cannot bring about such change by themselves, create the open intellectual climate necessary to produce individuals who are creative and self-confident, and who are more likely to work for such change. He applauds the work of Brazilian educator Paulo Freire, and others who have already initiated such revolutionary approaches to education as he recommends.[35]

The specific kinds of changes upon which he bases his hopes for a better future include the taming and humanizing of technology, the improvement of environmental quality, a revitalization of politics through a renewal of participatory democracy, the containing of the influence of computers, a revival of communities, and others.[36]

For Robert Jungk, the theoretical aspects of the future are far outweighed by the practical. The task to which he addresses himself is one of stimulating participatory popular action to create a better future. Comparing him to the three other European futurists represented above, it is possible to see a steady progression from theory into practice, with each in turn displaying a comparatively greater belief in human power and responsibility to shape the future.

Futurism in the United States

The study of the future in the United States, though more recently developed than its European counterpart, has made significant advances during the past fifteen years. This section will further attempt to define the concepts of futurism through an examination of the writings of individuals whose works are generally recognized as representative of futurist thinking in the United States.

These six include a journalist (Toffler), two sociologists (Bell and McHale), an economist (Theobald), a physicist and "think tank" director (Kahn), and an engineering professor (Harman). The term "futurist" can be applied to each of these individuals, as they have all become increasingly concerned with the study of the future.

Alvin Toffler and Anticipatory Democracy

To Alvin Toffler goes the major share of the credit for making the American public aware of the futurist perspective. His book *Future Shock*[37] and three other publications[38] have done much to raise the public consciousness about this field. He has been an effective publicist for the idea that we are suffering from the effects of rapid change.

Future Shock is a journalistic tour of a wide variety of manifestations of the author's contention that we are living in a period of unprecedented and accelerating change which has led to the psychological malady stated in the title.

Toffler is essentially a popularizer and a publicist for the futurist perspective. He has, however, contributed significant ideas to two major themes: anticipatory democracy, and the attempts to anticipate future values.[39]

Toffler defines anticipatory democracy as an approach to the long-range future which stresses "vastly increased popular participation and feedback."[40] This process can be manifested in a wide variety of ways, he suggests, such as the creation of city or statewide "2000" organizations (such as Iowa 2000); movements which involve the participation of workers, women, minorities, the elderly, and the poor; community action programs, and others. The basic premises of this anticipatory democracy revolve around: (1) the idea of management by developing a more positive attitude toward planning,

and (2) reversing the trend in which most individuals feel they are powerless to control their political institutions.[41]

A second major idea of Toffler's concerns the fact that anticipating, planning for, and making decisions for the future will involve the imposition of present values upon those who will be living twenty, fifty, or a hundred years from ·now. He raises the question of how we can anticipate future values.

Daniel Bell and the Post-Industrial Society

Daniel Bell, well-known Harvard sociologist and chairperson of the American Academy of Arts and Sciences Commission on the Year 2000, has been a major figure in giving academic respectability to the study of the future. He has also been a significant contributor to an understanding of the concept of the "post-industrial society," which is said to occur in a period of history which he feels Western society is entering at the present time.[42]

This post-industrial society, of which the United States will experience the full emergence in the next thirty to fifty years, will be characterized by: (1) an increasingly greater emphasis on providing services, rather than on providing goods, (2) the increasing pre-eminence of the professional and technical class, (3) the increasingly central function of theoretical knowledge in promoting innovation and policy-making, (4) control over technology, partly with the aid of technology assessment, and (5) the increasingly greater use of scientific personnel, computers, etc., in decision-making.[43]

Above all, Bell's approach to the future is one of the best examples of linear, extrapolative thinking, in which he assumes that we can predict things to come with reasonable degrees of certainty with the expectation of few major surprises. He looks toward the year 2000, and even to 2100, with the unemotional detachment of the social scientist basing his conclusions on available data. He does, however, recognize that the outcomes of predictions are determined not by trends acting in isolation from one another, but by their interacting as interdependent systems.[44]

Herman Kahn and Establishment Optimism

Perhaps the most optimistic of contemporary American futurists is Herman Kahn, former physicist and director of the Hudson Institute, one of the country's leading "think-tanks." Primarily, Kahn is an advocate of the "technological fix." That is, he believes that the solutions for today's major problems—e.g., food shortages, disease, unemployment, etc.—lie in the applications of science and technology to whatever ends appear most immediately appropriate. Like Bell, Kahn relies heavily on statistical data to supply the raw material from which he makes extrapolations of trends and other predictions.

Kahn and his associates are also responsible for the formulation of "The Long-Term Multifold Trend of Western Culture," which is an attempt to use the data from a wide variety of sources to provide a comprehensive overview of what he believes the next several decades will bring.

Kahn suggests that this trend is going to continue throughout the world, although some aspects of it are not necessarily beneficial nor desirable.[45] In this and in other forecasts of things to come in the 1970s and 1980s, Kahn uses what he terms "surprise-free projections," which are projections of coming events which would not be surprising to the forecaster if they should occur.[46] They are arrived at by analyzing theories and extrapolating trends, but are assumed to be wrong to some extent. Their purpose is to serve as a framework for the analysis and discussion of the trends, and for a consideration of the feasibility or desirability of alternatives.

The quintessence of Kahn's attitude toward the future can be found in his re-

cent work, *The Next 200 Years,* in which he presents a scenario which suggests that by the year 2176 the earth will have a population of fifteen billion people, with a $20,000 per capita income, and people will have completed their conquest of nature.[47] He recognizes that the problems of overcrowding, famine, resource scarcity, pollution, and poverty cannot be dismissed; but he sees them as only temporary or regional phenomena which can be solved in the near or medium-term future through the application of science and technology. He believes that the resources of the earth are more than sufficient to sustain increased living standards for greater numbers of people through economic growth, which can continue indefinitely.[48]

He also envisions a technological "wonderland" of innovations, such as floating cities and industrial complexes, space colonies, and technological breakthroughs which will supply us with inexhaustible sources of energy and raw materials. Economic growth will, however, begin to slow and will eventually reach a state of equilibrium, not because of imminent shortages, but because humanity's basic needs will finally be satisfied.[49]

The food supply problem and pollution will also be solved by applications of new technologies. Although Kahn concedes that there may be some occasional setbacks and even catastrophes, he feels that the eventual transition to a super-industrial society is inevitable.[50]

Robert Theobald and the Communications Era

Robert Theobald is a prolific writer on future-related topics, and the founder of a bimonthly periodical devoted to the exchange of future-oriented ideas within which he has organized a futures resources and information network.[51] Of his major theoretical contributions to the futures field, the ones which stand out are: (1) his characterization of the historical period we are entering as the "Communications Era," and (2) his development of processes whereby individuals can exchange ideas and information which will enable them to take more active roles in the creation of change.

Those who extrapolate present trends, he suggests, and forecast either a pessimistic or an optimistic future, are closed to the possibility of creative alternatives.[52] The coming of the Communications Era, according to Theobald, is being marked by a shift of emphasis from the industrial sector of the economy to the communications sector. This communications sector involves "the entire range of activities that exist to move information," ranging from the multiple uses of computers, to the increasing pervasiveness of mass media, to education, as well as to the trend to create more effective intercommunication among people.[53]

Theobald believes that we can and must change the direction in which we perceive society heading; i.e., from "the industrial era based on power, competition, production and transportation, to the cybernetic era based on cooperation, process, and information movement," and from centralization to decentralization. But to do this we must first perceive the nature of the basic contradictions with which we are living.[54]

He also suggests that we are living in a historical period which requires us to act "in ways never previously achieved by societies." To do so, we must overcome the barriers to change, such as societal constraints and inertia, and "find out how to create massive change."[55]

Theobald has been a moving force behind efforts to encourage individuals to interact with one another in two ways: (1) by publicizing opportunities for people to get directly involved in a wide variety of activities for creating change and working for reform, and (2) by helping to establish idea exchange networks among concerned individuals across the United States, wholly outside of any institutional structure, in which useful dialogues and possibly active involvement can be facilitated.[56]

Like Alvin Toffler, Robert Theobald is an advocate of broad-based popular participation in dialogues and debates on the issues which will help to determine the shape of the future. He believes that the people can effect changes significant enough to alter the pessimistic projections which some have extrapolated from present trends.

John McHale, Social Invention, and Experimentation

To the late sociologist John McHale, the future will not be simply a continuation of the past, but will be something radically different. This is strongly suggested by the rate at which society is changing. We must recognize, however, that human intervention now plays an unprecedented role in shaping the future. With the powers available to them, human beings increase the number of alternative futures available, as well as increasing the range of possible consequences of their actions. This power to shape the future is also a major factor in legitimizing the study of the future and in leading to the creation of agencies devoted to predicting and planning for increasingly long-range programs.[57]

Social futures, though also more open to alternative possibilities than ever before, are subject to the collective will, and therefore involve such elements as power, influence, politics, professional expertise, and bureaucracies.[58] The debate over social futures is therefore most complex and less accessible to the individuals in the society. This area is therefore more likely to be the domain of the "experts" and professionals. This, said McHale, is a situation which obtains as a result of the growing numbers of professionals engaged in futures research, which is already overbalanced in favor of technological, economic, and military projects. Moreover, the various alternatives which are considered are usually tied to the traditional values and goals of the society that tend to be reflected by many futures researchers (and/or by those who provide the funding for such research).

McHale recognized that "our collective futures tend to be oriented toward those models and scenarios that receive public attention and support." What is needed, therefore, is: (1) broad public understanding and participation in future-oriented explorations and discussions, and (2) resistance to the overprofessionalization of futures research, or its "division into a number of intellectual provinces cultivated only by their respective expert elites."[59]

McHale placed himself in opposition to those who continue to cling to the more traditional values and virtues in the face of revolutionary change. These traditional attitudes, he said, "are inadequate guides to the future, serving mainly to perpetuate old inequities and insecurities." Instead, we must become more consciously experimental and innovative. Our highest priority, he said "lies with social invention—the re-evaluation and redesign of our social forms and possibilities."[60]

Experimentation with new forms of individual and cooperative relationships, with innovative social organizations, and with new styles of decision-making must not be considered deviant forms of behavior, as is often the case. They are necessary responses to a world which has been made into one interdependent global community by scientific and technological realities. He suggested that we must transcend value systems based on obsolete concepts and vested interests of particular groups, and instead adhere to values based on a global-ecological ethical imperative, which combines a concern for the environment as well as for the "have-nots" of the world.

To a great extent, McHale suggested, the immediate future is predisposed by the recent past—our social institutions which are designed to transmit values from the past, and the socialization process which is designed to "assume a measure of continuity of conceptual orientation and social attitudes." In changing the future, therefore, we may also have to change our views of the past. "Traditionally, the value of the past was to supply stability and continuity to the present, but its more critical relevance lies in identifying within our past historical conditioning those attributed constraints that endanger and obscure our future possibilities. The need is not to cut ourselves off from the past so that we can achieve the future, but to review past potentials and disabilities in the light of those changed conditions that give us a greater range of choices and options."[61] He further suggested that a re-evaluation of the past may even be a more important priority "than the elaboration of more futures."[62]

Willis Harman and a Coming Transformation

Willis Harman believes that Western society is approaching one of the great transformations in human history, from industrial society to what he calls "trans-industrial society", in which ecological and self realization values will become dominant.[63]

Harman is a scholar who, as director of the Center for the Study of Social Policy at the Stanford Research Institute, has devoted many years to the study of the systemic changes occurring in society. In elaborating an approach for the study of the future, he suggests that we must confront directly the possibilities for radical change, and their implications, even though they may appear threatening to the status quo. By thoroughly understanding the forces which are transforming our world, he says we may be able "to move with them" rather than resisting them to the point of disaster.

Futures research, he suggests, can enable us to understand the forces of change and thereby to deal more effectively with them.[64] This understanding can be facilitated by recognizing the patterns which social systems tend to follow:

1. Social systems exhibit continuity. They change gradually rather than abruptly. Development is evolutionary.

2. Social systems tend to be "internally consistent." Generally, there are few if any contradictions among the various sectors of a society.

3. The similarities in fundamental characteristics among social systems can lead to the use of anthropological and historical models in studying the future. In other words, events in other cultures and at other times can be studied for their possible parallels to today's situations.

4. The study of past cause and effect connections or statistical correlations can facilitate an understanding of things to come.

5. Social systems can be viewed holistically in viewing the process of evolution and change.

6. Social change is not aimless. Societies tend to move toward goals.[65]

Harman's primary interest is with delineating the nature of the transformation he believes is an imminent possibility for Western civilization. In describing the factors involved in this possible transformation, he adopts the perspective of Kuhn's classic study of paradigms.[66] Using Kuhn's definition, Harman reports that society's "dominant paradigm . . . is largely embodied in the unquestioned, tacit understanding shared by people in that society and is transmitted not through overt 'teaching' but through the exemplara encountered in everyday life."[67]

We are presently living, Harman believes, during the waning stages of the dominance of the industrial-era paradigm, which consists of: (1) industrialization, productivity, and increasingly higher standards of living, (2) an emphasis on science and technology, (3) a belief in unlimited material progress, and (4) the predominance of pragmatic values in which individuals are free to pursue their own interests irrespective of what is good for the society.[68]

This paradigm, although it has been responsible for the extraordinary material successes of industrialized societies, has also led to a number of dilemmas which are not resolvable within the present paradigm or mindset. Harman mentions five failures of the industrial-era paradigm: "1) It fails to promote one of the most fundamental functions of a society; namely, to provide each individual with an opportunity to contribute to the society and to be affirmed by it in return. 2) It fails to foster a more equitable distribution of power and justice. 3) It fails to foster socially responsible management of the development and application of technology. 4) It fails to provide goals that will enlist the deepest loyalties and commitments of the nation's citizens. 5) It fails to develop and maintain the habitability of the planet."[69]

Harman goes on to suggest that there are signs of a new paradigm emerging that would have the following characteristics: (1) a perception of the inadequacy of the values upon which the industrial era paradigm has been based, (2) a re-orientation of science toward guiding the evolutionary development of humanity and society, and emphasizing understanding rather than generating more manipulative technology, (3) an emphasis on "being" rather than on "having" or "controlling," (4) an embodiment of an ecological ethic, and (5) an incorporation of a teleological view of life and evolution (as having direction and purpose).[70]

The future, Harman suggests, is far from being certain with respect to this transformation. If accomplished successfully, it could amount to one of the most significant transformations in history. It is also possible, however, that the transformation will fail to materialize, and the industrial-era paradigm will remain dominant. Still another possibility is that a transformation is in fact under way, but that resistance to it will cause a general breakdown of the system. He believes that a period of chaos ahead seems inevitable, "as the powerful momentum of the industrial era is turned in a new direction and the various members and institutions of the society respond at different speeds."[71]

The implications of Harman's thoughts are perhaps the most sobering of all those examined in this section on futurists and their ideas. The purpose of this brief examination of futurist ideas, however, has not been to determine their possible validity or soundness, but rather to illustrate the ideological, topical, and methodological range of approaches which exists in this field of study.

Futurism: The Need for Synthesis

We began this chapter by noting the natural aversion of people to reflect upon the future. It was hypothesized that one reason such thought is avoided is that it tends to produce anxiety over an uncertain future. If this hypothesis has validity, then what of the individual who does begin to study and reflect upon the concept? Donald Michael warns us of the consequences of future thinking as a threat to competence by noting that "Trying to think seriously about the future poses (a) challenge to one's sense of competence [because] additional complex and unfamiliar information must be absorbed and incorporated."[72] As one delves into dimensions of the future, one is forced to seek structures and frameworks by which to organize and categorize new information. To do this, one must isolate the basic postulates and then fit new information into this framework as perceived appropriate. It is likely that much restructuring and reorganizing will be part of the process. Though futurism is

only emerging as a field of endeavor, a number of efforts aimed at identifying basic postulates and providing organizational structures have appeared. In the following section we will attempt to delineate some of these postulates and structures.[73]

Toward a Philosophy of Futurism[74]

Edward Cornish asks the question "Do Futurists have a unique perspective on the world? If so, what are its underlying assumptions?" In responding to an implicit "yes" to the first question, he identifies three underlying assumptions which he states as emerging principles. These are: "1) the unity or interconnectedness of reality, 2) the crucial importance of time, and 3) the importance of ideas, especially ideas about the future."[75] In elaboration of the unity principle, he notes "An insistence on the interconnectedness of everything in the world, including the human race in all its manifestations, and in the impossibility of fully comprehending any single entity without considering its place within the whole. . . ."[76] Such thinking is called holistic. On the time principle, he notes that futurists recognize that present-day problems are the product of our past and are the result of gradual change through time. Therefore, futurists, while concerned with the present, tend to focus on the period from five to fifty years ahead.[77] The final principle is "The Importance of Ideas." Cornish notes that ". . . ideas or *futuribles* are critically important because our thinking is shaped both by our concepts of what happened in the past and our images of what we may see in the future. Ideas are the tools of thought."[78]

Norman Henchy provides a tentative framework to help point out relationships between the methods, goals, and assumptions of different futurists.[79] To do this Henchy poses and answers the following questions:

1. What are the different kinds of futures and the different kinds of statements that can be made about the future?

Possible Futures: what *may* be. This involves creating scenarios and describing alternatives, arising from the arts, history, and anthropology.

Preferable Futures: what *should* be. This involves proposing images of man [humankind] and the future, arising from philosophy, theology, social criticism, and utopian literature.

Probable Futures: what *will likely* be. This involves projecting trends and arises from our knowledge of history and the social sciences and our use of forecasting methods.

Plausible Futures: What *could* be. This involves producing policies and it arises from systems theory, planning activities, and operations research.

The objectives of futures studies emerge to be:

To expand the range of *possible* and *plausible* futures to extend our areas of choice and our areas of control;

To define and clarify the content of *preferable and probable* futures so that both our goals and our tendencies may become better understood;

To increase the area of intersection (i) between *preferable* and *plausible* futures to integrate our powers with our values, and (ii) between *preferable* and *probable* futures to integrate our goals and our trends.

2. What kinds of assumptions must a futurist make?

A. Assumption About Time (for *possible* and *probable* futures)

1) The Meaning of the Present
We are living in a period that is essentially continuous/discontinuous with the past.

2) The Nature of Change
Social change in its broad outlines follows a pattern of evolution/progress/flux/preordained destiny/cycles/spirals.

B. Assumption About Hope (for *plausible* futures)

3) The Degree of Confidence
In general, we are optimistic/pessimistic about the future.

4) The Possibility of Control
Man is basically able/impotent to shape his destiny and avoid disaster.

5) The Style of Intervention
It is necessary to conserve/reform/radically alter our basic institutions and ways of life.

C. Assumptions About Perceptions (for *preferable* futures)

6) The View of Reality
Natural and social reality is fundamentally a construct of our minds/something with an independent existence/basically meaningless/a useful tool for man if he adapts to it.

7) The Nature of Man
To be human is to be free/determined/good/bad/naked ape/machine/spirit.

8) The Reliability of Knowledge
Knowledge is an objective truth that we discover/a subjective interpretation that we invent.

9) The Importance of Values
There must be value commitment/detachment in our assumptions and analysis.

10) The Criteria of Significance
The dilemmas and their resolution are best seen as essentially political/economic/historical/philosophical/religious/scientific/technological/ethical/ . . .

3. What are the different approaches to the study of the future?

4. What are the major methods for studying the future?*

Approaches	Methods
Philosophical	Image Building Systems Building
Scientific	Policy and Planning Forecasting
Historical	Trend Analysis Comparative Studies
Artistic	Scenarios Insight

5. What are the relationships among these kinds of futures, assumptions, approaches and methods?

(See pattern on the following page)**

---

*For elaboration, it is suggested that the article be consulted. See note 73.

**Used with permission of the author and the World Future Society.

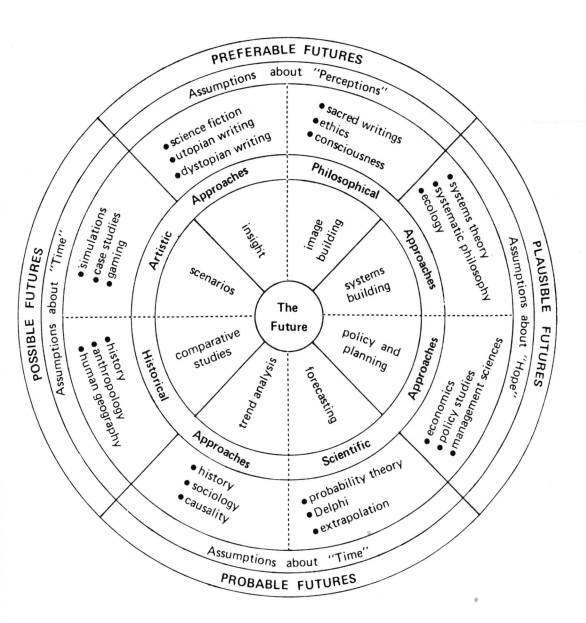

Using the architectural premise of Frank Lloyd Wright, Roy Amara suggests that "form should follow function in structuring the futures field."[80] Amara has suggested three basic functions: (1) to facilitate the formation of images and goals for the future, (2) to provide the necessary analytical and methodological tools with which to explore and influence the direction of human affairs, and (3) to advance participatory social planning.[81]

Futurism: Parameters of the Field

An examination of definitions, ideologies, and methodologies reveals a fair number of broad generalizations which may be helpful in delineating the parameters of this field of study:

1. Futurism is primarily concerned with enlarging and extending social perspectives, and with developing better and more sophisticated ways of thinking about the future.

2. With the growing number of scholars and increasingly sophisticated methods becoming associated with the study of the future, futurism is becoming an academically respectable perspective.

3. Futurism is concerned with predictions and forecasts about the future. But, more importantly, futurism is concerned with helping individuals develop understandings, attitudes, and abilities which in turn can help them deal more effectively with change and with the social responsibilities of living in a technological society.

4. Futurism is based on the premise that the future cannot be accurately foretold, but it can be conceptualized in a number of different and potentially useful ways.

5. Futurism is based on the belief that since the activities of humanity are coming to have increasingly long-range and global consequences, a more careful study of those possible consequences is necessary.

6. Futurism is the study of alternatives. It is based on the idea that there is not one future but many possible futures, with individual and collective choice playing important roles in influencing the actual future which occurs.

7. Futurism is also deeply involved in facilitating an understanding of change. Its development has been a direct response to accelerating change and the consequences of such change on the individual and on society.

8. Applied futurism is inseparable from theoretical futurism. Both are concerned with identifying and acting purposely to promote the realization of desired goals.

9. The subject matter of futurism is not restricted by the traditional boundaries of the academic disciplines. It is an interdisciplinary perspective.

10. Futurism is also identified with the attempt to understand and explain the relationships within and among the complex systems of which the natural and social worlds are composed; e.g., the nation-state system, the ecological system, economic systems, etc.

11. A strong component of futurism is a global orientation based on the belief that we live in a finite and interdependent world which requires conservation, cooperation, and peace.

12. Another strong component is the ecological perspective which reflects a deep concern over the various threats to the environment.

13. Methodologically, futurism is based on a wide variety of techniques and processes for analyzing probable, possible, and preferable developments. By being grounded in concepts from statistics and social science, and by being validated not by the ability to facilitate successful prediction, but by permitting the examination of alternatives, consequences, and goals, futurism is becoming increasingly legitimate.

14. Futurism includes a wide variety of ideological persuasions. By using the future as a conceptual perspective through which these persuasions can be viewed,

they can be made to stand out in sharp contrast to one another. This is made possible by conjectures about the possible short- and long-range consequences of different types of human behaviors and actions.

15. Although there are many pessimistic scenarios about the future, futurism is basically optimistic. Much of the literature is based on the attitude that, though problems of great magnitude exist, human intelligence can be applied in more deliberate ways to deal successfully with them. In many cases this notion has led to the desire for the increased use of planning to achieve desirable futures and to avoid undesirable ones.

16. Although much of the literature about the future stresses scientific and technological futures, an increasingly significant component focuses on the non-technological humanistic aspects of the future.

17. Finally, futurism is a new perspective which may be able to facilitate a more complete understanding of the present. It can be regarded as a diagnostic tool that may add to our insight about the nature of the world in which we presently live.

What of the Educational Response?

If, as some futurists indicate, we are experiencing one of the great discontinuities in history and are beginning a societal transformation, what, then, of our educational response? As noted by one author, "One of the glaring ironies of modern education is that the schools try to prepare students to live in a time that does not yet exist by concentrating their studies on a time that has ceased to exist."[82] In past times of slower change the task of education was to conserve the past and to present it to each subsequent generation. Such a task made sense when the future could reasonably be expected to be like the present. While the times have changed, our educational response has

not. Social education must respond to new realities.

Notes

[1]Alvin Toffler, *Future Shock* (New York: Bantam Books, 1971, 1970), p. 10.

[2]Fritz Perls, *Gestalt Therapy Verbatim.* (Lafayette, Calif.: Real People Press, 1969).

[3]Benjamin D. Singer, "The Future-Focussed Role Image," in Alvin Toffler, ed., *Learning for Tomorrow* (New York: Vintage Books, 1974), p. 19.

[4]Edward Cornish, "What Shall We Call the Study of the Future?", *The Futurist*, Vol XI, No. 1. February 1977, p. 50.

[5]Plato, *The Republic*; Ernest Callenbach, *Ecotopia* (New York: Bantam Books, 1977); Sir Thomas More, *Utopia*; Sir Francis Bacon, *The New Atlantis*; St. Augustine, *The City of God*; Robert Owen, *The Book of the New Moral World* (New York: G. Vale, 1845); Samuel Butler, *Erewhon* (New York: Signet, 1872); Edward Bellamy, *Looking Backward 2000–1887* (Boston: Ticknor, 1888); H. G. Wells, *A Modern Utopia* (New York: Chapman and Hall, 1905); Aldous Huxley, *Brave New World* (New York: Harper & Row, 1932); George Orwell, *1984* (New York: Harcourt, 1949).

[6]Ossip Flechtheim, "Is Futurology the Answer to the Challenge of the Future?", in Robert Jungk and Johan Galtung, eds., *Mankind 2000* (Oslo: Universitesforlaget, 1969), p. 264.

[7]*Ibid.*

[8]*Ibid.*

[9]Ossip Flechtheim, *History and Futurology* (Meisenheim Am Glan: Verlag Anton Haim, 1966), p. 65.

[10]*Ibid.*

[11]*Ibid.*

[12]*Ibid.*

[13]*Ibid.*, p. 79.

[14]Bertrand de Jouvenel, *The Art of Conjecture* (New York: Basic Books, 1967), pp. 18–19.

[15]*Ibid.*, pp. 4–5.

[16]*Ibid.*, p. 5.

[17]*Ibid.*, p. 10.

[18]*Ibid.*, pp. 18–19.

[19]*Ibid.*, p. 18.

[20]*Ibid.*, pp. 25–26.

[21]Fred L. Polak, *Prognostics*, (Amsterdam: Elsevier, 1971), p. 305.

[22]*Ibid.*, p. 248.

[23]*Ibid.*, pp. 248–250.

[24]*Ibid.*, pp. 254–260.

[25]*Ibid.*, p. 306.

[26]Fred L. Polak, *The Image of the Future* (San Francisco: Jossey-Bass, Inc., Publishers, 1973), p. 5.

[27]*Ibid.*, p. 19.

[28]Fred L. Polak, "Responsibility for the Future," in Robert Bundy, ed., *Images of the Future* (Buffalo, N.Y.: Prometheus Books, 1976), p. 11.

[29]Polak, *The Image of the Future*, p. 23.

[30]Robert Jungk, "Toward an Experimental Society," in Bundy, *Images of the Future*, p. 138.

[31]Robert Jungk, *The Everyman Project* (New York: Liveright, 1977), p. 36.

[32]Robert Jungk, "Human Futures," *Futures* I (September 1968), p. 38.

[33]Jungk, *The Everyman Project*, p. 72.

[34]*Ibid.*, p. 73.

[35]*Ibid.*, p. 80.

[36]*Ibid., passim.*

[37]Alvin Toffler, *Future Shock* (New York: Random House, 1970).

[38]Alvin Toffler, *The Futurists* (New York: Random House, 1972); *Learning for Tomorrow* (New York: Random House, 1974); *The Eco-Spasm Report* (New York: Bantam Books, 1975).

[39]Alvin Toffler, "What Is Anticipatory Democracy?", *The Futurist* IX (October 1975), pp. 224–229; Alvin Toffler, "Value Impact Forecaster—A Profession of the Future," in Kurt Baier and Nicholas Rescher, *Values and the Future* (New York: The Free Press, 1969), pp. 1–30.

[40]Toffler, "What Is Anticipatory Democracy?", p. 224.

[41]*Ibid.*, p. 227.

[42]Daniel Bell, *The Coming of Post-Industrial Society* (New York: Basic Books, 1973).

[43]*Ibid.*, p. 14.

[44]Daniel Bell, "The Study of the Future," *The Public Interest* I (Fall 1965), p. 124.

[45]Herman Kahn and Anthony J. Weiner, "The Use of Scenarios," in Alvin Toffler, ed., *The Futurists*, p. 9.

[46]*Ibid.*, p. 40.

[47]Herman Kahn, et al., *The Next 200 Years*.

[48]*Ibid.*, p. 27.

[49]*Ibid.*, pp. 31, 69–105.

[50]*Ibid.*, p. 1.

[51]*Futures Conditional* (periodical).

[52]Robert Theobald, "Educating People for the Communications Era," in Richard W. Hostrop, ed., *Foundations of Futurology in Education* (Homewood, Illinois: ETC Publications, 1973), p. 4.

[53]Robert Theobald, *Beyond Despair* (Washington, D.C.: New Republic Book Company, 1976), p. 4.

[54]*Ibid.*, p. 6.

[55]*Ibid.*, p. 14.

[56]Robert Theobald, letter to author, July, 1977.

[57]John McHale, *The Future of the Future* (New York: George Braziller, 1969), pp. 3–4.

[58]*Ibid.*, pp. 10–11.

[59]*Ibid.*

[60]*Ibid.*

[61]*Ibid.*, pp. 20, 29.

[62]*Ibid.*, p. 29.

[63]Willis W. Harman, *An Incomplete Guide to the Future*. (San Francisco: San Francisco Book Co., 1976), p. 3.

[64]*Ibid.*, p. 7.

[65]*Ibid.*, pp. 11–14.

[66]Thomas S. Kuhn, *The Structure of Scientific Revolutions* (Chicago: University of Chicago Press, 1962).

[67]Willis Harman, "The Coming Transformation," *The Futurist XI* (February 1977), p. 5.

[68]Harman, *An Incomplete Guide to the Future*, p. 25.

[69]*Ibid.*, pp. 27–28.

[70]*Ibid.*, pp. 32–33.

[71]*Ibid.*, pp. 34–36.

[72]Donald N. Michael, *On Learning to Plan—And Planning to Learn* (San Francisco: Jossey-Bass Publishers, 1973). p. 160.

[73]Edward Cornish "Towards A Philosophy of Futurism," *The Futurist*, Vol. XI, No. 6, pp. 380–381. Also see: Edward Cornish, *The Study of the Future* (Washington, D.C. World Future Society, 1977), pp. 96–102. Roy Amara, "The Futures Field: Functions, Forms, and Critical Issues," *Futures*, August, 1974. Mark Anderson, "Time: How Do Futurists Perceive It?", *World Future Society Bulletin*, Vol. XI No. 3, May-June 1977, pp. 15–21. Norman Henchy, "Building a Framework for the Study of the Future," *World Future Society Bulletin*, Vol. XI, No. 5, Sept.-Oct. 1977, pp. 1–9.

[74]Cornish, *The Futurist*, Vol. XI, No. 6, p. 380.

[75]*Ibid.*, p. 380.

[76]*Ibid.*

[77]*Ibid.*

[78]*Ibid.*, p. 381.

[79]Henchy, *World Future Society Bulletin*, Vol. XI No. 5, pp. 1–8.

[80]Roy Amara, "The Futures Field," *Futures* VI (August, 1974).

[81]*Ibid.*, p. 290.

[82]Ronald T. LaConte, *Teaching Tomorrow Today* (New York: Bantam Books, 1975), p. 5.

2.
Curriculum Approaches to Teaching About the Future

We will employ the name *futures education* to designate what has become a fairly broad range of approaches used to translate selected concepts and techniques of futurism into learning experiences suitable for elementary and high school students. Although no accurate figure is available, the existence of hundreds of such programs across the United States has been documented.

Collectively, such attempts to provide instruction about the future have been labeled a "grass roots" movement, because individual classroom teachers have been largely responsible for taking the initiative for designing such units, courses, and other approaches to the future as seemed appropriate to the particular settings involved.

Such efforts have naturally been characterized by considerable diversity in quality, sophistication, and content:

A program in the Richfield-Burnsville, Minnesota schools, for example, entitled "Futuristics: Theory and Application," attempted to get students to become more systematic and objective in their understanding and creation of alternative images of the future. Included in the course were units on a comparative study of several futurists and their ideas about the future, technology and its role in the future, and responses to technology and change. Students in the course were also given intensive practice at using several forecasting methodologies, as well as being given the opportunity to work as interns with some individual in the community who was actually engaged in some relevant type of future-oriented work.

In the Shaler Area Schools in Glenshaw, Pennsylvania, for a course entitled "The Future," students were taught that: (1) there are major differences between a "fortune-telling" approach and the academic-professional study of the future, (2) we can hypothesize or create images of alternative futures, and (3) those hypotheses can be studied as possible, probable, and preferred futures.

The basic goals for a course entitled "21st Century" in Nordonia High School, Macedonia, Ohio, included: (1) "To view the future in a meaningful framework, the growing edge of the present, and not as an area of limbo and endless surprises." (2) "To point to the rights and responsibilities of a citizen as he plans for a new life style in a society undergoing rapid change." and (3) "To be aware that some past assumptions may no longer be valid due to such things as the technology revolution."

In Ardmore, Pennsylvania, students were offered a course entitled "Computers, Society and the Future," in which they studied the possible impact that computers and other forms of technology may have on our future. A major component of the course consisted of field trips to various museums, computer centers, hospitals, and businesses where they could see the technologies they were studying in actual operation. The course also included a wide variety of readings in science fiction and non-fiction, films, guest speakers, and the actual construction of a simple computer.

In Parma, Ohio, several social studies teachers collaborated on a mini-course

Just take a superficial look at history and see whether the course of future events would not have been better perceived in broad outline if more study had been devoted to the future itself.

—Fred Polak

which they entitled "Worlds in the Making (Futuristics)." The units of study included: Coping With Change; The Role of Technology; Life Styles; Work and Leisure Time; and Age of the Mind (an examination of paranormal abilities such as ESP). A major aim of the course was to have the students examine some changes and alternatives in a selected number of fields, so that they might identify some future possibilities and their likely implications. A frequent discussion catalyst in the course consisted of "What If" situations that the students were asked to consider.

Why Teach The Future?

Schools have been called upon to pursue a number of goals in order to "properly" educate the young. One of the more recent of these demands has been a call to return to the "basics." But precisely what is "basic" for a society in which change has become such a common feature? According to many observers, we have entered into a transitional period in history, the outcomes of which cannot be discerned. Just what are the basic skills, understandings, and attitudes which will have the greatest potential value for ensuring our survival through these next tumultuous decades? We cannot answer these questions in any absolute sense. Undoubtedly, the three R's will remain essential for some time to come, but even now their position is being challenged by the growing importance of becoming fluent in the various computer languages. Computers, television, videodiscs, and other electronic innovations may soon diminish the stress placed on being literate in the traditional sense.

Beyond the development of basic skills, particularly in the social studies curriculum, what can we identify as having continuing significant potential for facilitating the process of socialization, and for developing an "educated" citizenry? We recognize the value of history, for example, for giving students an understanding of their cultural heritage and traditions, and for allowing them to gain a sense of perspective in time and space. Similar arguments can be made for the continuing importance of studying government, economics, sociology, geography, and other subjects. They each serve in a specific way to familiarize the student with basic societal concepts and inquiry processes, the understanding of which aids the furtherance of socialization and cultural continuity.

As supporters of futurism in the curriculum, however, we believe there is an additional dimension of time, besides the past and the present, to which we must attend. By adding a future dimension to the learning process, we help to provide direction, purpose, and greater meaning to whatever is being studied. By integrating past, present, and future we act to strengthen a neglected link in the learning process. For students who will spend perhaps two-thirds of the remainder of their lives in the twenty-first century, such a future orientation in education may be quite basic indeed—particularly since that future is almost certain to be radically different from the present.

Another element in a rationale for teaching the future lies in the need to help students develop skills and abilities for dealing with increasing societal complexity. It appears to have become necessary to provide students with new tools and perspectives through which they may develop greater competencies in dealing with long-range issues, in becoming more skilled at managing the exponential growth of information, and in becoming more insightful in sorting out social priorities and moral issues.

The major issues today—nuclear proliferation, pollution, global scarcities, etc.—require the sound application of understandings, logic, compassion, and informed value judgments in order to make wise decisions. By teachers adding a future dimension to students' intellectual skills, such issues may come into sharper focus. By attempting to determine the possible long-range implications of personal actions or public policies, students analyze additional data in the decision-making process, increasing the likelihood that such decisions will be based on what may be best for coming generations and not what is merely expeditious for the present one.

By confronting students with novel issues and problems, instruction which is oriented toward the future may reduce the element of surprise in students' confrontation with change. By being helped to become informed about undesirable societal trends and their alternatives through the projection of such trends into the future, students may begin to develop a greater sense of social consciousness than seems to be the norm at present.

Such students may develop into citizens who are more likely to become involved in debates over public issues and in other forms of political activity. They may be more likely, having been steeped in the longer-range perspectives of futures thinking, to take initiatives in directing their own lives toward purposeful goals, as well as in participating in activities designed to promote alternative societal trends aimed at more desirable futures.

Finally, it appears to be important to teach about the future in order to facilitate the development of attitudes and skills which are more appropriate to the times in which we live. We need, for example, to emphasize learning strategies which develop creative and imaginative thought processes, rather than methods which emphasize little more than the acquisition of facts. Problem-solving skills, inquiry, and the use of a range of techniques developed by futurists play major roles in futures education. Though inquiry has long been a goal of social studies education, the study of the future may provide additional strength to the implementation of inquiry strategies.

As with any innovation, however, many variables intervene between theory and practice. Successful efforts to develop future-oriented understandings and skills require the fulfillment of several criteria, including teacher expertise and skill, administrative cooperation, and parental support.

Some Characteristics of Futures Education

With such a diversity of perspectives involved in the futures education movement (of which the above examples are only a very small sample), and with its development still in a stage of infancy, the characterization of this innovation by a number of generalizations may be a risky undertaking. We offer the following, however, with the disclaimer that certainly not all programs conform to these perceptions. Indeed, some of the following generalizations may be said to more accurately represent the *potential* of the futures education movement, rather than its actuality at the present time.

1. Futures education encompasses a range of subject matter from many disciplines and sub-disciplines. History, economics, government, geography, sociology, psychology, biology, ecology, technology, and many other areas are

represented. The result of this convergence of subject areas is an essentially interdisciplinary approach wherein issues are often studied in a more or less integrated manner. This integration permits the study of the world holistically, without regard for the boundaries of the disciplines that often interfere with the complete understanding of issues.

2. Futures education represents an attempt to persuade students to think more systematically about the future. It is an effort to help them develop what Benjamin Singer calls a "future-focussed role image," which is our self-image projected into the future.[1] The development of such a perspective in young people, it is claimed, will help to stimulate future-oriented motivation and achievement.

3. Since it deals largely with the hypothetical and the problematical, futures education is heavily weighted toward the use of inquiry strategies and problem-solving techniques. In large measure, these approaches are very familiar to social studies educators. A major distinction in futures education, however, is the addition of a number of methods with considerable potential for generating and processing data in rather unique ways. Specifically, we are referring to a number of forecasting techniques which are featured in many futures courses. Foremost among these (explanations will be provided in the following chapter) are Delphi polling, trend extrapolation, futures wheels, relevance trees, cross-impact matrices, dynamic modeling, and scenarios. Not only do these techniques facilitate the processing of data in new and potentially exciting ways, but they teach students a number of specific skills which can be later applied to other situations.

4. Another aspect of futures education is its open-endedness. Some teachers may still attempt to impose facts and predetermined conclusions upon students, but the possibility of this occurring would seem to be significantly reduced in futures courses. The teacher is placed in the position of not having the certainty of knowledge which characterizes the traditional teacher-student authority relationship. It is not true, however, that one answer is just as good as another. Rather than being the fountainhead of knowledge from which the students come to drink, the teacher becomes a facilitator in the development of logical thinking skills, the correct applications of data, and problem-solving abilities, as well as a stimulus for hypothesis-making, imagination, creativity, and informed speculation. In other words, although traditional memorization and recitation procedures are unlikely in futures courses, their absence does not imply that such courses lack intellectual rigor or substance. The crucial variable in such courses remains the teacher.

5. Although concerned to some extent with forecasting the future, a major intended outcome of futures courses is the development of insight and perspective into the major issues of today, the outcomes of which will shape the future. There is no evidence to suggest that futures courses are not firmly anchored in the realities of the present. The message usually comes through loud and clear. *What we do today will determine the shape of tomorrow; therefore we must carefully weigh the possible implications of our present behaviors and actions.*

6. Many futures courses also contain a strong value component, either explicitly or implicitly. Our attempts to shape the future are grounded in our value systems. Changing conditions and perceptions during the present era may be adding up to some fairly profound changes in our most cherished values. Consider the following equation: hard work + economic growth = progress = affluence = the good life. Clearly, there are some basic challenges arising to the assumptions underlying these value indicators. Based on the writings of some futurists, the follow

ing equation may emerge in the years ahead as a replacement to the one above: simple living + appropriate technologies = selective economic growth = an equilibrium society = the good life.

If nothing else, futures education represents an opportunity to re-examine the possible implications of our continued adherence to certain values versus the possible implications of a shift to alternative values, particularly those which may be more likely to ensure our continued survival in the years ahead.

7. Another major characteristic of futures education is a high degree of optimism. There appears to be an implicit consensus supporting the belief that societies will eventually solve the major dilemmas with which they are confronted. The doomsday thinking which characterizes some futurist writings does not appear to be a feature in any of the futures courses we have seen. Instead, a faith in human efforts to find viable solutions to world problems—particularly technological solutions—appears to be the dominant perspective. Some of the literature, however, has begun to stress a skepticism toward such technological solutions and to suggest more visionary alternatives. In time, futures education may also come to mirror some of this skepticism, and to provide insights into some of the alternatives.

8. Many futures courses attempt to help students understand the distinctions among the concepts of possible, probable, and preferable futures. For example, the possible future may be studied by reading science fiction, through the use of brainstorming and other forms of speculative thinking, and through the use of student-written scenarios. The probable future may be examined by studying trends and other forms of exploratory projections. The preferable future may be studied through cross-impact matrices, impact analyses, attitude surveys, value analyses, and other subjective methods.

9. A major feature in the literature about futures education is the idea of creating, through such courses, individuals who will be more likely to take initiatives in managing the future, rather than allowing events to take them by surprise. This has been referred to as the development of a "pro-active" orientation as opposed to the re-active orientation which most of us possess. This pro-active orientation is characterized primarily by a high degree of self-motivated behavior which is dominated by the realization that desirable futures will not evolve automatically; we must work together to make them happen. Participation and involvement must occur in order to make the future what we want it to be.

10. Finally, futures education is not dominated by any particular topic or issue, but frequently includes instruction related to the following themes: environmental problems, energy alternatives, global issues (e.g., the search for world order, third world development, population and food supply), the promises and hazards of technology, the effects of change, and others.

Alternative Organizational Frameworks

Up to this point, we have been describing futures education in the sense of its representation by separate courses in the curriculum. The separate course approach, however, is only one of three possible ways in which instruction in futures education might be organized. The other two approaches are: The separate unit on some future-related topic added to a standard social studies course, and the "infusion" approach where future-oriented ideas and concepts are more or less integrated into the standard curriculum. The following examples will illustrate how all three approaches might be designed:

Outlines of Separate Courses in Futurism

Example #1: "Toward the World of Tomorrow"

I. The Study of the Future
   A. Major Futurists and Their Ideas
   B. Predicting and Forecasting the Future
II. A World in Crisis—Pessimism vs. Optimism
   A. Environmental Alternatives—Does Nature Know Best?
   B. Energy Alternatives—The Limits to Growth
   C. Population and Food—The Neo-Malthusians
III. Technology—Solution or Part of the Problem?
   A. Bigger Is Better vs. Small Is Beautiful
   B. Is There a Computer in Your Future?
   C. Space Colonies and Cosmic Pilgrims

Example #2: "Exploring the Future"

I. Why Study the Future?
   A. Can We Predict?
   B. Can We Make a Difference?
II. The Effects of Accelerating Change
   A. Future Shock—Transcience, Novelty, Diversity
   B. Adapting to Change
III. Case Study: "The Long-Term Multifold Trend"
IV. Automation, Work, and Leisure in the Future
V. Social Relationships in the Future
VI. Meeting Basic Needs—Food and Shelter Alternatives
VII. Can We Shape the Future?

Separate Units
Within Standard Social Studies Courses

The separate unit within standard social studies courses can add a futures dimension to the curriculum without having to confront the problem of adding an additional course. The topics included here are only initial suggestions. Perusal of futurist literature will yield many additional possibilities.

Example #1: American History Units

1. "Images of America in the Year 2000"
2. "Toward America's Tricentennial"
3. "Social Change and the American Future"
4. "New Frontiers for the Next Thirty Years"

Example #2: World History Units

1. "A Future for Europe (Africa, Latin America, Asia, etc.)"
2. "Prospects for Global War or Peace"
3. "Is There a World Government in Our Future?"
4. "Projecting World Trends: Social, Political, Economic"

Example #3: Sociology Units

1. "The Future of the Family"
2. "Changing Life Styles for the Future"
3. "Work and Leisure in the Year 2000"
4. "Women's Roles in the Year 2000"
5. "Designing Social Change"
6. "The Future of Mass Communications"

Example #4: Government/Civics Units

1. "What Is Anticipatory Democracy?"
2. "Government and Politics in the Year 2000"
3. "Futurists in Congress Today: Planning for Tomorrow"
4. "Citizen Participation To Shape the Future"
5. "The Future of Race/Minority Relations"
6. "Designing a New Constitution for the Year 2000"
7. "The Future of Federal-State Relations"
8. "Bigger Government or Decentralization in the Future?"

Example #5: Economics Units

1. "The Coming of a Post-Industrial Economy"
2. "Energy and the Economy of the Future"
3. "The Economic Thought of E. F. Schumacher"
4. "Environment, Energy, and Jobs"
5. "A Superabundant Economy or a Coming End to Affluence?"
6. "Assessing the Possible Effects of a No-Growth Economy"

Example #6: Psychology Units

1. "Adapting to Rapid Change"
2. "Psychosurgery and Mind Control"
3. "A Coming Psychochemical Society?"
4. "The Psychology of Prediction"
5. "Creativity: The Mind Designs the Future"

Example #7: Anthropology Units

1. "The Future: Beyond Culture"
2. "The Anthropological Implications of Space Colonization"
3. "Cultures from Other Worlds"

These could be units of a week or longer in duration, or they could be topics to be discussed in only one or two class sessions. They give only a brief illustration of the alternatives for orienting standard social studies courses toward the future. Many more possibilities can be generated by reading futurist literature relating to each particular discipline.

Integration or Infusion

A third way to futurize the curriculum is to integrate ideas, concepts, and methods of futurism wherever they can be made to fit the topic or issue being studied. Betty Barclay Franks and Mary Kay Howard, writing in the January, 1979 issue of *Social Education,* have already provided some excellent examples for "infusing" standard social studies courses with future-oriented ideas.[2]

Since all subject areas relate to the future in some way, it stands to reason that many, if not most, could be taught with a future-orientation. In some cases this would not be appropriate, however, because the shift of time perspective might detract from the task of getting students to master the fundamental ideas of a subject.

The fundamental aim of the infusion approach is to integrate past, present, and future so that students become used to considering all three time dimensions together. In addition to applying past, present, and future concepts wherever possible, frequent use of various forecasting techniques can serve to infuse futurism into the curriculum.

In large part, however, successful infusion of futuristic ideas and concepts depends upon the teacher's abilities, perceptions, and familiarity with the futures perspective. The teacher must be on constant lookout for appropriate topics and issues in which to inject activities, strategies, and discussion questions which relate to the future. The following are some suggestions for getting started:

● In history courses, for example, it is possible to identify individuals who had certain visions of desirable futures, in support of which they pursued certain policies and goals. Political leaders, religious leaders, inventors, writers, entrepreneurs, and others had visions and dreams which they pursued in various ways. How, for example, did they attempt to express and/or implement their visions? Where did they succeed or fail? How might the present have been different had they pursued alternative visions or policies? How might the present have been different had they not been born, or had died prematurely? How did the pursuit of their visions alter the course of events? What are the possible relationships between visions or images of the future and the course of history? What kinds of images of more desirable futures do we have today?

● Students might be asked to write scenarios of alternative futures which might have evolved from the pursuit of different goals over the years. They could make futures wheels by projecting the effects of actual events from the time they occurred to the time their effects were actually felt by society. The cotton gin, the reaper, the radio, the automobile, and television are examples of technological innovations for which students could create past/futures wheels. (The following chapter contains instructions for the design of this technique.)

● Other standard social studies courses, such as economics, sociology, government, psychology, and geography, generally have a more present orientation. To infuse them with a futuristic orientation involves going a step or two beyond an examination of current conditions to an analysis of trends and prospects for the future. This can be done through the use of forecasting techniques and through the frequent use of magazine and journal articles to supplement text materials. The most useful periodical is *The Futurist,* but *U.S. News & World Report, Saturday Re-*

view, *Psychology Today, Time, News-week,* and many widely available magazines frequently publish articles on trends and other future-related issues. Daily newspapers are also frequent sources of information about trends and proposals and could be used extensively.

It is important, in attempting to actually futurize such courses, to transcend the traditional "current events" approach and structure whatever inquiries are pursued into systematic investigations into the future—the possible, the probable, and the preferable. The identification of long-range implications of current situations and trends for the next ten, twenty, or thirty years can also facilitate this process.

Notes

[1]Alvin Toffler, ed., *Learning for Tomorrow* (New York: Random House, 1974), p. 21.

[2]Betty Barclay Franks and Mary Kay Howard, "Infusing a Futures Perspective into Standard Social Studies Courses," *Social Education* 43 (January 1979), pp. 24–27.

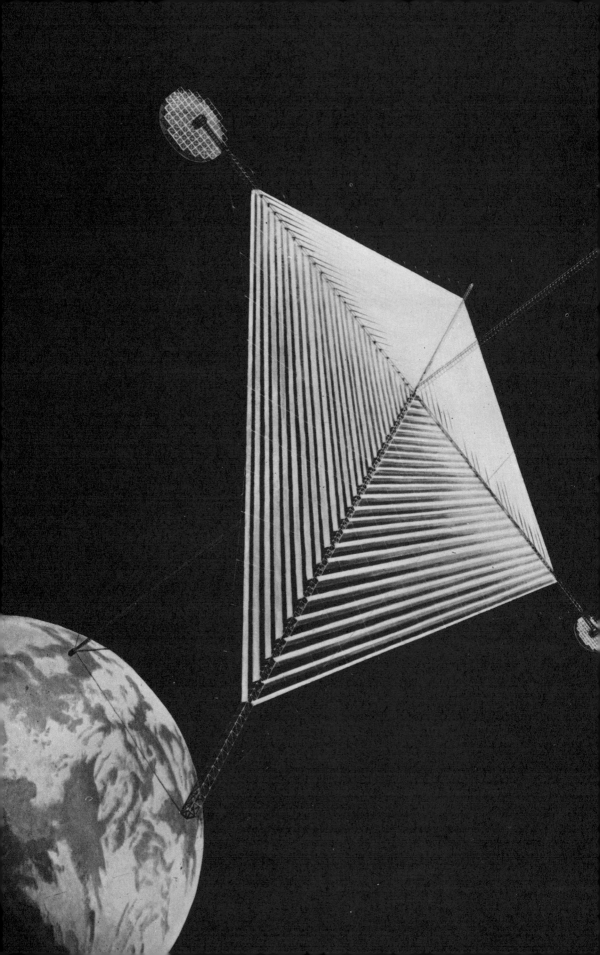

3.
Innovative Methods for Teaching About the Future

Teaching and learning about alternative futures can be an exciting and rewarding endeavor for both teachers and students. As with teaching any subject, however, enthusiasm should not be regarded as the sole criterion of effectiveness. To teach about alternative futures effectively requires a clear conception of desirable goals, a reasonable amount of familiarity with the literature, familiarity with a range of forecasting techniques and other strategies, the identification of appropriate student materials, and a plan for designing and integrating courses and units.

In addition, the teacher must be willing to do whatever is necessary to create a classroom climate where students are encouraged to think creatively and imaginatively, and where they can feel free from the evaluative judgments so often imposed on their expressed thoughts. Ideally, a balance must be struck between the attempts to encourage rigorous, logical thinking, and attempts to elicit thinking which may seem illogical or nonconformist at first glance, but which may contain elements of wisdom and/or originality. The teacher must refrain from such comments as: "That couldn't possibly work." "Let's be more realistic." "That goes against our basic values." "It would be too costly." Or other such put-downs.

Thus, a major element in designing or creating the future is the encouragement of imaginative or visionary thinking, qualities which are far less likely to emerge in an atmosphere of scorn or ridicule. Of particular importance is the task of eliciting ideas which may appear impossible or impractical. We must transcend what Arthur C. Clarke has called "the failure of nerve," and "the failure of imagination" in order to encourage originality in thought and courage in expression.

Goals for Futures Education

The initial task in developing an approach to teaching the future is to identify possible goals and objectives. Naturally, a single course cannot accomplish more than a small number of broad goals. Each teacher must therefore identify those which seem most appropriate to the needs of the particular setting. As futures education programs expand, more goals and objectives can be included. The following goals represent a broad range of possibilities for adaptation to particular courses and units.

1. Students will understand that we cannot predict the future but we can investigate the potential implications of various alternative futures.

2. Students will understand that the seeds of the future are contained in the present. What we do today will influence the shape of tomorrow.

3. Students will understand that in order to shape the future in positive ways we must carefully weigh the implications of the alternatives open to us.

4. Students will understand that we can create mental images of alternative futures. Positive images may become personal or societal goals. Negative ones may help us to identify actions and policies we must avoid.

5. Students will understand that by identifying current trends our efforts to

*Through education's reliance on deductive thinking, its fear
of the creative, subjective and inductive thought processes,
its demand that students merely regurgitate what the
professors and textbooks say, it has ingrained people
into thinking that they cannot handle anything new.
The only ideas that seem valid are ones that are based on
an extrapolation of the past.*

—Robert Theobald

forecast the future may become more specific and concrete.

6. Students will understand that the act of forecasting the future may itself become the source of a self-fulfilling or self-defeating prophecy as we strive to approach or avoid its fulfillment.

7. Students will understand that we are all partially responsible for what happens in the future—through our votes, our life styles, our patterns of consumption, and our overall value systems.

8. Students will understand that technological innovations play major roles in determining the rate and direction of change.

9. Students will understand that the world must be considered as a single, interacting global system, and humankind must be viewed as a single human community.

10. Students will understand that the past, present, and future are all related to one another, and that each time perspective should be studied for the contributions it can make to an understanding of the other two.

11. Students will be able to identify and analyze various trends, which may or may not continue into the future for various reasons.

12. Students will be able to identify various ways in which individuals can have an influence on the future.

13. Students will be able to use and apply a variety of forecasting methods in

analyzing future-related problems, issues, and trends.

14. Students will be able to develop hypotheses or images of the future.

15. Students will be able to identify the major futurists and analyze some of their most important contributions to futurist thought.

16. Students will be able to analyze critically and evaluate both pessimistic and optimistic forecasts of the future.

17. Students will demonstrate the development of an attitude of responsibility toward the future by their actions.

18. Students will be able to evaluate the possible effects of anticipated changes on their own personal goals and projected life styles.

19. Students will be able to identify the ways in which they can anticipate and adapt to change.

20. Students will be able to identify the ways in which they can become more actively involved in influencing their own futures.

Using the Methodologies of Futurists

One of the popular notions in the literature of the past decade on teaching the social studies is that of having students do what it is a historian or social scientist does when he/she is practicing his/her field of endeavor. The underlying premise is that the student learns the skills relevant to the discipline and thereby learns how to learn. Futures education provides abundant opportunities for the continuation of this practice and, in fact, extends the potential of such endeavors by adding intuitive, visionary, and speculative dimensions. As with other aspects of futures education, it is necessary for the teacher to use caution in achieving balance between the possible, the probable, the plausible, and the more fanciful applications of these methodologies. Still, when used with such caution, the methodologies of futurists are highly useful devices for classroom application.

Predicting and Forecasting

It is not an exaggeration to say that the futurist would like to be able to predict the future, but he/she knows that it is not possible. Under such circumstances the logical alternative is to make the most informed statement of probability that is possible. Thus a significant distinction is made in futurism between predicting and forecasting the future. Roy Amara notes that one of the most common misconceptions about futures research is that the primary objective is to predict the future.[1] Forecasting provides a systematic and formal means for determining future possibilities which goes beyond speculative conjecture. It is a system of quantified estimates of change and alternative possibilities. To make forecasts the futurist utilizes a wide range of methods. Dickson has suggested the existence of some 150 methods and techniques, of which only a dozen or so are in general use.[2] Forecasters seek to identify patterns of behavior and to use these patterns to anticipate future behavior. In the final analysis, the application of these methodologies is aimed at assisting in intelligent decision-making.

Joseph Martino divides forecasting methods into two basic kinds—"exploratory" and "normative." Exploratory methods begin with the present and its history, and attempt to project future developments. Normative forecasts start with some desired or postulated future and work backward seeking paths of transition from the present to the postulated future.[3]

This distinction is an important one for teachers applying these methodologies in their futures work. Exploratory forecasts are more concerned with probable and plausible futures while normative forecasts are more concerned with desirable or preferable futures. In this connection it is also useful to make a distinction between those methodological techniques which are used to instruct or to encourage investigation of other circumstances or conditions which may affect forecasting and the actual forecasts themselves. These techniques, which Etzioni calls "heuristic futures," are intellectual games or exercises seeking insights into what might happen if an event were to occur or certain circumstances were to prevail and are to encourage the exploration of alternatives.[4] In examining methodologies the element of time must also be considered. Some forecasting methodologies deal with long-range probabilities and possibilities while others deal with short-range futures.

In the section which follows we will briefly describe some of the techniques that futurists utilize in forecasting the future. Following the descriptions we will discuss the utilization of these techniques in the classroom. Finally, we will provide some examples of classroom applications.

Techniques for Forecasting the Future

• *Trend Extrapolation Forecasting* is a technique based on the assumption that events, circumstances, or developments which have occurred over time past will continue into the future and therefore will provide some insight into possible futures. This technique is a form of projection which has elements based on different assumptions. For example, one may assume that the future will be like the past (persistence forecasting) and that the rate of change will be constant as in the past (trajectory forecasting). Or one may assume that a past cyclic pattern will continue. Another dimension of trend forecasting may be the assumption of causality in that events or occurrences are associated with each other. Finally, there may be the assumption that some trends may be analogs for other trends and hence serve as models. Trend forecasting has perhaps its greatest use in anticipating the near future and requires refinement through the addition of other techniques.

• *The Cross-Impact Matrix* is a form of Matrix forecasting which provides the basis for conjecture as to how several trends, occurrences, or events may impact each other. The cross-impact matrix is a means for considering how all interacting forces are likely to help shape the future. It clarifies underlying assumptions and is especially useful in revealing errors and/or inconsistencies. The matrix may be a simple one involving only one set of variables which are placed on both a horizontal and vertical dimension, or it may be a more complex matrix involving two or more sets of variables. A sample cross-impact matrix will be found below.

• *Delphi Forecasting* is a technique of polling knowledgable opinion regarding expectations of possible alternative futures. The procedure involves polling and repolling experts regarding likely trends or developments. After each poll the results are refined, seeking greater consensus and specificity of the trends or developments under consideration. Thus Delphi probes are a form of intuitive forecasting which may seek to estimate the timing of future events, the routes change may take, or future problems, needs, or opportunities. They are usually conducted through anonymous questionnaires.

Cross-Impact Matrix

How do the variables posited affect each other?

	Gasoline Rationing	Air Pollution	Mass Transit	Inflation
Gasoline Rationing		reduced air pollution as fewer miles driven	favors growth of mass transit as public has less gasoline	reduced inflation due to less money being spent for expensive foreign oil
Air Pollution	produces incentives for gasoline rationing		favors growth of mass transit as fewer autos are driven, producing less pollution	necessitates more expensive pollution control devices for autos causes auto costs to rise
Mass Transit	reduces need for gasoline	reduces air pollution		could produce more inflation due to less cost of mass transit
Inflation	?	could reduce air pollution due to cost of driving	produces need for less expensive public transport	

• *A Futures Wheel* is a device for assessing the internal consistencies of trend forecasts. An idea, trend, event, etc. is placed in the center of a page and lines are drawn outward, with each line ending in a possible result or association with the initial idea. The process is then continued from each succeeding association so as to create second, third, and fourth order consequences of the initial idea. A futures wheel is illustrated below.

• *The Scenario* is another popular futurist technique. The scenario is a narrative description of a posited future. The writer simply projects and describes some future condition or state of affairs and then explains the relevant variables or circumstances. It is an interesting creative way of presenting a possible future, and the process of creating a scenario provides the writer (and the reader) with a means of examining alternatives and the consequences of decisions. The scenario utilizes other forecasting techniques so as to refine the projected alternative future. Also, scenario writing forces the creator to examine her/his underlying values and assumptions which shape decisions involving the final product. Similar to the scenario, but with one major difference, is the *future history*. The future history is an attempt to trace the possible development of events leading up to a particular state of affairs in the future. It is a chronological explanation of hypothetical circumstances that might lead up to a future point in time when the scenario takes place. As noted above, the scenario and future history are often combined in a single narrative.

FUTURES WHEEL

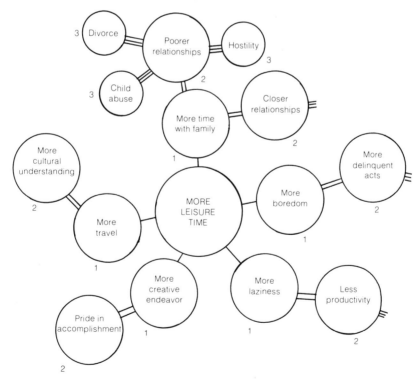

• *The Relevance Tree* is a form of goal-oriented forecasting which utilizes a network of alternative pathways for reaching predetermined future goals. It is important to note that with this technique we have made a shift to a normative conception. In many respects the relevance tree is a form of planning how to reach a preferred future or avoid an undesirable one. Thus the relevance tree becomes a tool for locating constraints and critical decision points in achieving an agreed upon future goal. The relevance tree is constructed by placing the present situation on one side of a page and the sought goal on the other. The possible alternative actions to achieve the goals are then branched out from it, and then each alternative means of achieving that branch is placed out from it. A sample relevance tree is found below.

• *Simulation Forecasting* involves the use of models which simulate a future and are used to predict future probabilities. These often involve the use of computers and they may be utilized for their analytical potential or in the classroom for instructional purposes. A good example of such a simulation for classroom use is the Limits to Growth model which involves the use of trend projection.

These brief descriptions and examples of some of the more widely used and popular forecasting techniques are only to illustrate the potential of futurist methodologies for the development and/or enhancement of a wide variety of thinking skills in the classroom. The teacher who desires to use these or other techniques in the classroom will wish to study them in detail. A word of caution is in order on this point, since these techniques as they are

Sample Relevance Tree

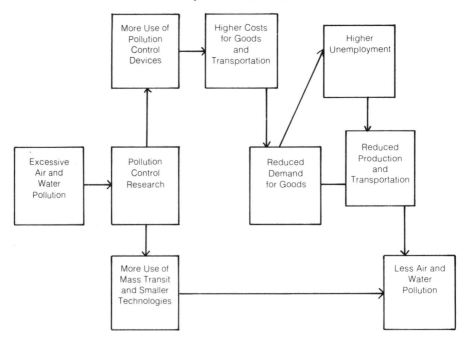

applied by futurists are very sophisticated and extremely complex. For use in the classroom it is necessary to adapt and simplify them. Most books which survey the futures field contain sufficient description of the basic elements to allow the interested teacher to create her/his own adaptation. A number of books on this subject will be found in Chapter Eight, and we have found Hencley and Yates' *Futurism in Education*[5] to be especially useful.

Brainstorming and Creativity

A major intended outcome of futures education is an increase in the ability of students to think more creatively and imaginatively. Brainstorming is an excellent technique for stimulating creative thinking when its possibilities are fully exploited. Among the most important rules for using brainstorming are:

1. Do not take time to evaluate ideas as they emerge. Be non-judgmental and simply record them. Suspend criticism.

2. Encourage "far-out" and wild ideas. Such "off-beat" suggestions may not be practical in themselves, but they may trigger other more useful ideas.

3. Encourage quantity. The more ideas which emerge, the greater likelihood that some of them will be useful.

4. Encourage "piggy-backing" on one another's ideas in order to produce new combinations and possibilities.

Other ways to encourage creativity can be applied when using the above forecasting techniques or when having students perform other activities. There are various checklists for stimulating creativity, and many other practical suggestions, in the booklet *Have An Affair With Your Mind*, edited by Angelo M. Biondi, and published by Creative Synergetic Associates, Ltd. of Great Neck, New York.

A Sampler of Futures Activities

Teaching the future certainly does not require the exclusive use of completely novel methods. Most standard activities can be used: readings, films and other media, panel discussions, position papers, guest speakers, field trips, student presentations, games and simulations, group projects, lectures, demonstrations, etc.

The following activities provide a few illustrations of additional ones which can be used to elicit student reactions to various future-related problems and possibilities. With a little imagination, the teacher can devise similar ones to fit the particular topics or issues which are to be dealt with.

1. Model City

Purpose: To have students identify alternative ways in which human needs might be served in an urban setting.

Procedure: Tell students they are to design a self-contained model city to house approximately 50,000 people, in which all the basic services (police, recreation, health care, shopping, waste disposal, water, power, etc.) are provided. Students may be given large sheets of heavy paper and felt tipped pens to make their drawings, and they are divided into several groups.

Each group could then be given different requirements and constraints under which to work. Some possibilities are: The city must recycle all its wastes; it must supply all its own power; it must be pollution-free; it must take up no more than one square mile of land area; all parts of the city must be easily accessible by mass transit. Other conditions, hypothetical innovations, or constraints can be added by the teacher.

After drawing their city, each group could then present it to the rest of the class and answer questions about the reasons for its design.

2. Technology Boom

Purpose: To have students understand the degree of technological growth during the past twenty years.

Procedure: Have students compile individual lists of things created by technology which we did not have ten years ago. A second list, prepared perhaps with their parents' help or by looking through old magazines, could identify those things which were not around twenty years ago.

Presentations of those lists could lead to a discussion of the nature of progress, the quality of life now as opposed to then, and the prospects for further changes in the next ten to twenty years.

3. We Create the Future

Purpose: To have students brainstorm alternative responses to the following problems in order to invent new solutions that have not been tried yet.

Procedure: Have students come up with as many ideas as possible regarding the following problems:

a. Develop new uses for garbage.

b. Suggest alternative ways to dispose of toxic chemicals and nuclear wastes.

c. Develop new ideas for mass transit systems.

d. Develop alternatives for competitive sports.

e. Suggest new ways to conserve diminishing resources, such as fresh water, oil, etc.

f. Suggest incentives for getting people to become more ecologically conscious and concerned about the future.

g. Suggest alternative uses for television and radio.

h. Suggest alternatives to compulsory education.

4. The Good Old Days

Purpose: To help students gain a sense of perspective in identifying and evaluating changes in society which contribute to progress, and those which bring new problems.

Procedure: First, have students read one or two accounts of everyday life in America between 1900 and 1920. Have them identify what we mean by the term "the good old days." What was good about them? What was not so good? In what ways are we better off today? In what ways are we not as well off? Can we have the "good'" things without the bad? Do you think people fifty years from now will regard our present period as "the good old days"? Will people always look at the past with nostalgia and longing for things to be the way they used to be?

5. Time Capsule

Purpose: To have students identify and analyze the major characteristcs of our civilization as defined by our artifacts.

Procedure: Have students work in small groups in compiling lists of ten items they would wish to place in a time capsule in order to provide the people of a future time with an understanding of our own civilization. The time capsule would lie buried until the year 2500. A comparison of lists by the different groups could lead to an intense debate over which items most accurately represent our civilization, which items represent the best of our society, and which items represent the worst.

6. Help Wanted Ads of the Future

Purpose: To identify possible changes in the types of jobs which might be available in the future. Many present jobs will become obsolete and many new jobs and career opportunities will develop.

Procedure: Students are to write a help wanted ad for the year 2000 describing a job that does not now exist. They are to imagine possible changes in technology, products, and services, etc. They should also state the qualifications for the positions.

Next, they are to write a letter of application for this position, stating the reasons for seeking this type of employment and their qualifications for this job.

7. The Future of Leisure

Purpose: To acquaint students with a possible future situation which, though generally positive, might create some serious dilemmas.

Procedure: Tell students that leisure time in the future may increase markedly, with the introduction of more labor-saving devices and possible reductions in the work week.

Students are to assume that work will take only two hours per day by the year 2025. Sleep will require only three hours (due to electronic sleeping aids); and routine activities such as child care, housekeeping, commuting to and from work, shopping, etc. will consume perhaps three additional hours. This leaves approximately sixteen hours per day for leisure and recreational activities.

Students will be asked to describe some possible ways they would spend that time. The class can then discuss the possible implications of such a situation. Possible follow-up questions might include: Would such a life lead to new and creative ways to spend that leisure, or might it lead to boredom and depression? How do you think other people would use their leisure time? Would they use it to become better educated, or would they just waste it?

Students could also be asked to invent some future recreational activities and pastimes.

8. Interview—The Pace of Change

Purpose: To have students identify some of the possible effects of change.

Procedure: Have students interview their parents and/or grandparents to determine how much conditions have changed in their (the parents' or grandparents') lifetimes. They should especially seek to elicit their parents' reactions to the pace of change during the last forty years or so as they have perceived it.

9. Case Study—An Anti-Aging Pill

Purpose: To have students determine possible implications of an invention or innovation.

Procedure: This is the hypothetical situation: A drug company has developed an inexpensive pill which stops further aging from the time it is taken. A single dose lasts for one year, so it must be taken annually. It has no harmful side effects, and it is made from compounds which come from virtually inexhaustible sources. It has been fully tested and is ready to be marketed, pending approval by the Food and Drug Administration. Students are to role-play FDA committee members who must decide whether the drug is to be released or not. A yes or no decision must be accompanied by a rationale which fully explores the implications of the choice. In addition, if it is decided to release the drug, the FDA must also decide on what, if any, restrictions will be placed on its distribution. (Adapted from "The Immortality Game," by Joel A. Barker)

10. The Future Today

Purpose: To have students become aware of the frequency with which future-oriented topics are published in the media.

Procedure: Have students make a scrapbook of newspaper and magazine articles which reflect some trend or future-related issue. These could be classified under the categories of the possible future, the probable future, and the preferable future. They could be about a trend, a technological innovation, a plan for dealing with some issue, a legislative proposal, etc.

11. Marooned

Purpose: To sharpen students' perceptions of the nature of contemporary society, and their conceptions of change.

Procedure: Have students try to imagine that they have been marooned on a desert island for the last twenty-five years. Have them describe in an essay how they might react if they were suddenly found and brought back to civilization.

The students might be prepared for this exercise by being given a description of how things were twenty-five years ago.

12. The Good Life in 2001

Purpose: This is a values clarification exercise to determine how the students define "quality of life."

Procedure: Have students compile lists of living conditions, personal possessions, and personal relationships which would, for them, define the "good life" in the year 2001. Next, they could examine their lists to identify the things they prize the most.

13. CYBER IV for President

Purpose: To get students to evaluate the pros and cons of increasing control of society by computers.

Procedure: Students are told that a Constitutional Amendment in the year 2025 has passed, allowing the world's most advanced computer, CYBER IV, to run for President of the United States. This computer is so advanced that it will monitor all government operations and initiate its own orders to keep everything running smoothly, efficiently, and fairly. If elected, it will subject all citizens to its logical, unemotional, beneficent control.

Students are then to be divided into two groups, one to plan a campaign strategy to get CYBER IV elected, the other to plan a campaign to bring about its defeat. Having planned their strategies, the students could hold an election, perhaps involving other classes, or else they could simply present their arguments and conclusions in a final debate.

14. Future Lifestyles

Purpose: A values clarification exercise to have students project their desires into a future time frame.

Procedure: Students are invited to describe the life styles they would like to be living in thirty years, and to share those descriptions with their classmates. They could be asked to respond to the following questions: In what manner would you like to be earning your living thirty years from now? What kinds of activities would you be participating in? With what kinds of people would you be spending your leisure time? What kind of dwelling would you like to be living in? What other kinds of possessions would you like to have?

15. Futures Time Line
Purpose: To help students project personal and societal futures.
Procedure: Have students draw their personal timelines to the year 2050, indicating projected milestones such as marriage, children, education, jobs, awards, retirement, and death.

Next, they can make a second timeline to project societal futures during the same period.

They should then be asked to analyze the relationships, if any, between the two timelines to determine the possible effects societal projections might have on their projected personal futures.

16. Past, Present, Future
"The future of the past is in the future
The future of the present is in the past
The future of the future is in the present"
—*John McHale*

The future of the PAST PRESENT FUTURE ...is in the... FUTURE PAST PRESENT

Purpose: to help students speculate on the relationships between past, present, and future:
Procedure: The future of the ___ is in the ____.

Using the model provided, make three statements putting the words PAST, PRESENT, and FUTURE in the blank spaces.
Explain your choices. What are the implications of the statements for the study of the past, present, and future?

17. Development—Consequence Activity

Purpose: To get students to consider possible future developments and to hypothesize as to implication.

Procedure: A chart form of the following type can be utilized.

Description of the area of the development; e.g., Biological Breakthroughs		How likely is the result as a consequence of the development?				Effect of the consequence? (evaluation)				
Development If these developments were to occur:	Consequence they might result in:	Certain	Probable	Possible	Almost Impossible	Very Favorable	Favorable	Little, No Import	Detrimental	Very Detrimental
1. Chemical control of hereditary defects by gene modification through molecular engineering	A. increased life expectancy for people with such defects									
	B. government regulations relating to procreation									
	C. effects on genetic characteristics of next generation									
	D. —————									
2. etc.	A. etc.									

18. Conventional Wisdom Activity

Purpose: To encourage students to seek alternative ways of resolving societal dilemmas.

Procedure: List all of the "conventional wisdom," sayings, or advice one typically encounters, and change or modify it to make it functional for the future. What were the probable circumstances under which the statement was originally created? Explain why the statement may no longer be relevant. What values are explicit or implicit in the old and new versions?

19. Tree of Alternative Futures: Conceptualizing the Future Activity

Purpose: Some futurists have suggested that one way of conceptualizing the future is to think of it as a tree of possible alternatives.

Procedure: Make a sketch of a rather tall deciduous tree (why deciduous?) and consider this metaphor from the perspective of an individual climbing the tree. How would you label the trunk? The limbs? To think on the tree metaphor a bit more, would a palm tree make a good metaphor for the future? Why or why not? What sort of a society might be depicted by the growth of a palm tree?

Suggest other metaphors for conceptualizing the future. Explain your metaphor. Make a sketch of it.

20. Computer Talk

Purpose: Have students speculate upon the areas in our lives in which computers could handle tasks presently carried out by human beings.

Procedure: Construct a number of such messages from computers. How can an individual respond to such messages? What if the bill has been paid? How can errors be corrected? What if school tests and grades were all handled by computers?

```
LATE NOTICE


HI THERE I AM THE
   CREDIT UNION
     COMPUTER
   AS YET, I AM THE
ONLY ONE THAT KNOWS
THAT YOU HAVE NOT
PAID ON THIS
ACCOUNT. HOWEVER, IF
I HAVE NOT PROCESSED
A PAYMENT FROM YOU
WITHIN 10 DAYS, I
WILL REFER YOUR
ACCOUNT TO A HUMAN
FOR FURTHER CONTACT.
```

Using the Newspaper in Future Studies

An excellent but often overlooked resource for teaching about the future is the daily newspaper. Increasingly, newspapers are featuring articles and series devoted to various dimensions of future studies. Articles on technological developments and biological and psychological research, as well as on anticipated changes in societal institutions, tend to predominate. While there is a tendency for such articles to focus upon sensational or more extreme projections or predictions, such articles can be analyzed for the soundness of their ideas as well as being used to motivate more thorough study of the phenomenon under consideration.

To orient students to the newspaper as a source for future studies, one can begin by having students clip articles with the word "future" or other words which indicate a future-focus in the headline. These articles may be reported upon much as current events articles are used.

Scrapbooks may be kept and articles categorized as they relate to topics or issues under consideration. In reporting on such articles students should explain how the article is related to the future, whether it represents a trend, and whether it is basic and soundly researched. Headlines such as "What will your life be like in 2001?" are representative of the more obvious articles students will first collect. As students become more knowledgeable about futurism and its underlying rationale and premises, they will increase in their so-

Figure Out Future
environmental future
What will your life be like in 2001?
'insurance for future'
British now can read printed magazines on TV screens
Raising status of women to defuse population bomb

LEANER LIVING FOR AFFLUENT IS PREDICTED

TO THINK FUTURISTIC

U.N. UNIT WARNS OF 500 MILLION WHO ARE HUNGRY

Clones

Think Small
GAS

phistication as to the future-relatedness of articles which may not, on first glance, appear to have future implications.

Students must be taught to read from the futurist perspective by asking questions about what they read, such as "How is raising the status of women to defuse the population bomb?" "How is this related to 500 million who are hungry?" "Why is leaner living for the affluent predicted?" Students may utilize futures wheels to examine second, third, and fourth order consequences of events reported in articles. They may make cross-impact matrices of such events. After they study the future, the words "think small" may cause some students to think of the name of E. F. Schumacher and the concept of appropriate technology.

Often one finds intriguing futures-related "fillers" in the small spaces used to complete a column. The following is an example: How is this article related to changing life styles and changing values?

Faked own death

A geologist whose wife and two children hadn't seen him since his bloodstained van was found in the desert last year says he faked his own death to escape an unhappy home life and the "materialistic, status-seeking" world he lived in. . . . . , who was 39 when he disappeared last November, turned up this week in Eloy, Ariz., where he is living, with a waitress and working as a $1.25-an-hour cotton picker. He left behind his family, a $90,000 home in Palo Alto, Calif., and a $26,000-a-year job with the U.S. Geological Survey. . . . . . . said he is enjoying life as a common worker, although he plans eventually to return to geology.

Students may be asked to discern trends and developments related to fluctuation in the price of stocks of companies concerned with various technological capacities. Students could selectively "buy and sell" stocks based on their projections of technological, energy, or environmental developments. Students could engage in values clarification exercises by discussing whether the purchase and/or owning of stocks in companies which produce a detrimental environmental impact is a "good" thing or not.

The newspaper thus represents an excellent medium for establishing relevance and having students come to understand how seemingly diverse and unrelated events are frequently interconnected.

Additional Possibilities

• Have students list material possessions they would be willing to go without if they were convinced that their gesture would help ensure a better future for their grandchildren.
• Have students conduct interviews among teachers, relatives, and neighbors to determine their attitudes toward the future. The students could help design the questionnaires to be used.
• Have students design posters which reflect their images of the future.
• Have students draft a new Constitution for the year 2000.
• Have students put together a newspaper dated at some future date.
• Have students do reports on energy alternatives or ecological topics and report to the class.
• Have students interview local members of public interest, political action, or lobbying groups and report to the class on what these groups are trying to accomplish for the future.
• Have students read science fiction short stories and report on their meaning and possible significance for the future.
• Have students investigate some form of technology with which they are unfamilar and report to the class on how it works.
• Have students visit a city planning office, or have a city planner come to the class to explain how the future is created by people in the planning profession.

Notes

[1]Roy Amara, "Misconceptions About Futures Research and Planning," *World Future Society Bulletin,* Mar-April 1976, p. 3.

[2]Paul Dickson, *The Future File* (New York: Rawson Associates Publishers, Inc., 1977), p. 93.

[3]Joseph P. Martino, "Survey of Forecasting Methods," *World Future Society Bulletin,* November-December, 1976, p. 4.

[4]Amitai Etzioni, "Rules for Using Forecasts and Forecasters," *World Future Society Bulletin,* May-June, 1976, p. 10.

[5]Stephen P. Hencley and James R. Yates, *Futurism in Education* (Berkeley: McCutchan Publishing Company, 1974).

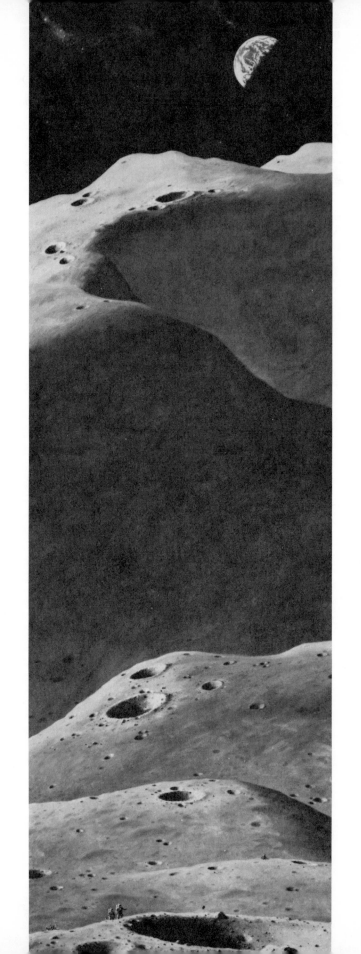

4.
Inquiry into Values and Futures Education

If the quality of life for the majority of us is not to deteriorate, far-reaching changes in human behavior must occur in the years immediately ahead.

Lester R. Brown, *World Without Borders*
(New York: Vintage Books, 1973), p. 113.

But in the end, the problems of the communal and post-industrial society are not technical, but political, for even though in the nature of the new complexities a large kind of new social engineering is involved, the essential questions are those of values. Only when men can decide what they want, can one move to questions of how to do the jobs.

Daniel Bell, *The Coming of Post-Industrial Society*
(New York: Basic Books, Inc.
Publishers, 1973), p. 337.

Socio-ethical decisions regarding the human condition need no longer be phrased in terms of what we can do—but in terms of what we choose to do, both individually and collectively.

M. S. Iyengar, in Alvin Toffler, ed., *The Futurists*
(New York: Random House, 1972), p. 191.

. . . there is a growing realization that man's future may be literally what he chooses to make it, and that the ranges of choice and the degree of conscious control which he may exercise in determining his future are unprecedented.

John McHale, *The Future of the Future*
(New York: George Braziller, 1969), p. 6.

Awareness of ideal values is the first step in the conscious creation of images of the future and therefore in the conscious creation of culture, for a value is by definition that which guides toward a "valued" future.

Fred Polak, *The Image of the Future*
(Amsterdam: Elsevier Scientific
Publishing Co. 1973), p. 10.

The real problem is to sort out the values that motivate our social and individual behavior, to analyze them clearly and profoundly, to uncover the conflicts between them, and then to choose, as consciously as we know how, which one to give precedence.

Alvin Toffler in Baier and Rescher, editors,
Values and the Future
(New York: A Free Press Paperback, Macmillan
Publishing Co., Inc., 1969), p. 26.

Values and the Future: On the Nature of Hard Choices, Difficult Decisions, and Potentially Disastrous Consequences

Rationale

In beginning our inquiry into values and the future, it is useful to remember that the basic reason for desiring to know more about the future is the utility of such knowledge in guiding present actions so as to anticipate, avoid, or resolve problems. Thus, our inquiry into values is concerned with recognizing how our values influence and shape the choices we make, choices which, in turn, create the future. It is true that we never escape our biases completely and that our cultural baggage influences us in ways that we often fail to recognize. Still, if we are to cope with the future with any degree of success, we must carefully analyze our value judgments in order to separate our built-in preferences from the demands of new realities.

Change, Choice, Decisions, Consequences. These key words, taken from the works of the above cited futurists, illustrate the overarching concern of futurism with questions of value. The future depends not upon our technological capacity to change, but upon our will to do so. The above quotations reflect the fact that people make choices and that these choices reveal their preferences which, in turn, mirror their values. Thus, what we value shapes our future. Our values are our guides: they function so as to assist us in making judgments of worth. It follows that if our values are based upon invalid premises, then our choices are unlikely to pro-

We can only pay our debt to the past by putting the future in debt to ourselves.

—John Buchan

duce the future we seek. It also follows that if, when faced with complexity and changed circumstances, we cannot determine value or choose from among competing values, we feel powerless, alienated, and isolated. We have difficulty in finding meaning in life.

How to get from here (the present) to there (the future) and to survive the trip is, in the final analysis, a question of values. Numerous futurists have addressed themselves to the problem of the apparent contradictions which exist between our present value system as it is popularly conceived and misconceived, and the requirements for successfully coping with the future. The issue is squarely joined by Robert Heilbroner in *An Inquiry into the Human Prospect:*

> How are we to deal with the elements of wish and fear, prejudice and bias, charity and malice that come flooding into an inquiry such as ours, threatening to divert it, despite our best intentions, toward some outcome that we favor from the start?[1]

Perhaps the most serious detriment to change is the tenacious (and fallacious) assumption that the future will be like the past and therefore what has worked in the past will work in the future. The main task for the teacher is to provide opportunities for the student to examine the basis upon which a particular value or set of values is held and to imagine new values which will allow for the creation of alternative future possibilities. Students must be made aware of the discrepancies which exist between their held values and the demands on those values which presently exist, or are likely to exist in the future.

These discrepancies can be made apparent as a result of providing relevant information and experiences. As the student acquires information and reflects upon the congruence or incongruence of his/her values with the information, the basis is laid for value change. To recapitulate: For the area of values and the future, one must begin by questioning the utility of our traditional values as guides for the future. From this point it is possible to expand one's analysis of values into an examination of possible new values to serve as guides for the future.

Selecting an Approach to Values and the Future

Over the past decade values education has received renewed interest as an area of endeavor in social education. As a recent phenomenon it reflects the ambiguities and confusion resulting from the translation of highly complex and abstract formulations into practical classroom strategies. Broadly stated there are three main areas of endeavor in the application of the concept of value in education. Among the approaches to value is the work of Oliver, Shaver, Newmann, and Berlak, which concerns itself with the role of value in the clarification of public controversy and the formulation of specific policy decisions.[2] Next, and clearly more popular with teachers, is the values clarification approach which focuses upon personal value clarification. Most widely known and used are the works of Raths, Simon, Kirschenbaum, and others.[3] Finally, there is the moral education effort resulting largely from the application of the

theories of Lawrence Kohlberg. While each of these areas in and of itself can present a reasonably well delineated approach to some dimensions of the concept of value, in classroom application they often seem to be indiscriminately mixed.

The future as an emerging area of study likewise presents special problems in its use of the concept of value. As we have indicated in our rationale, we prefer an approach to the concept of value that concerns itself with value as it is reflected in change, choice, decisions, and consequences. In this sense, the approach advocated here is most closely related to, and compatible with, the clarification of public controversy and specific policy decisions as advocated by Newmann and Oliver. Still, for values and the future, an important point for the prospective practitioner to keep in mind is the distinction between *an individual's values and broader social values* which are used to characterize a society. While it is true that the values of a given society are a reflection of aggregate individual personal values, futures education is best suited to the exploration of societal values.

Another complicating factor in futures education regarding the concept of value is that a substantial concern of futurism is dealing with value change—especially change resulting from notions of crisis and transformation. Finally, just as we can have no sure knowledge of the future, neither can we be sure of our value prescriptions. Thus, especially in the futures area we can obtain no immediate feedback on the actual outcome of a stated value preference.

Futures education, then, provides at various times opportunities to utilize all three of the approaches to values education cited above. We will not attempt to repeat the essence of these approaches here; the reader should consult the footnotes for the more popular works in these areas. Rather, we wish to make the case

for our approach to the value component of futures education, which makes for a more rational and a more personally fulfilling approach to teaching about values and the future.

Inquiry into Values

In the remainder of this chapter we will focus upon the element of choice and the assessment of consequences as a means of inquiry into values. The basic question is *"How can we make value choices?"*, and, for the transformation ahead, *"Which of our values must be modified and which way?"* Finally, we will propose the elements of a transformational ethic as a means of assessing the moral component of futures education.

Definition of Value

Baier defines a value as "an attitude for or against an event or phenomenon, based on a belief that it benefits or penalizes some individual group or institution."[4] Rokeach defines a value as ". . . an enduring belief that a specific mode of conduct or end-state of existence is personally or socially preferable to an opposite or converse mode of conduct or end-state of existence."[5] For our purposes the significant point is that focussing upon the value of a circumstance, event, social practice, or state of affairs views value as a certain sort of property. This allows for appraisal of the circumstance, event, etc. in terms of the definitions posed. Therefore, we undertake their appraisal in order to know the extent to which they are likely to satisfy the demands we make on them. We seek such knowledge because it is helpful when making rational choice involving these things.

Illustration

To illustrate, let us suppose that the Department of Energy asks the Congress for legislation which will impose fuel rationing. Thus, fuel rationing becomes the object of our value analysis. Let us further

suppose that legislation results which will impose a limit of two gallons per car per day. One then appraises this value object in terms of the definitions given. That is, what is the capacity of this legislation to confer benefit on someone and make a favorable difference to his/her life? Now, let us imagine that individual "A" lives 20 miles from his/her place of employment in downtown Los Angeles and owns a car that gets 16 miles to the gallon. Individual "A" initially appraises this legislation negatively; that is, he/she sees it as making an unfavorable difference to his/her life. But suppose that further events and/or information results from analysis of this circumstance. Car pooling arrangements are made by the employer or local government. Fast lanes are provided on freeways for car pool cars. The public transportation system is expanded and express buses serve the suburbs. Thus individual "A" can get to work more rapidly and at less cost than driving his/her own car. Further, it is demonstrated that the net result will reduce traffic by 35%, thus further reducing air pollution. Through nationwide media exposure it is shown that as a result of this legislation the nation will have to import substantially less foreign oil and that our balance of payments deficit will improve and that the rate of inflation will decrease. Thus, the individual in this case appraises this proposed legislation somewhat as follows:

Negative Effects	Beneficial Effects
1. reduced mobility/ flexibility	1. less wear on personal car
2. greater inconvenience	2. cleaner air
(a) scheduled car pool	3. less hassle from driving in heavy traffic.
(b) use of public transport	4. More disposable income
3. less fuel for recreation	(a) reduced cost of car pool or bus
(a) more T.V.	(b) car lasts longer—fewer repairs
(b) less chance to be with friends	
(c) more $ spent for cabs	(c) less $ lost to inflation
4. less status from car identification	5. contacts with more people; e.g., making new friends
5. contacts with more people; e.g., less privacy	

Obviously each list could be expanded, and each individual would view the situation differently depending upon personal values. Valences (+or−) could be attached to each item on the list and refinements made. First, second, and third order consequences could be projected through use of the Futures Wheel described on page 35. Importantly, such an appraisal can get beyond personal, individual values and extend into societal values, and thus confront the individual with conceptions of the greater good for the greater number.

Qualities of Appraisals

As in the case above, value is an evaluative property whose magnitude can be ascertained in appraisal. In determining magnitude we are assessing its capacity to confer benefit on someone. Baier calls assertions to the effect that something confers a benefit on someone a "meliorative" claim. Meliorative knowledge, then, is practical, applied knowledge.[6] As such, it has two elements: (1) being of benefit to someone, and (2) demonstration of the causal role in conferring the benefit. Appraisal of such claims is based on *how the change* affects the excellence of that person's life. In terms of futures education, then, we must regard the changes in a person's life as subject to his or her control and the outcome of choice. Thus the individual needs (1) relevant meliorative knowledge, and (2) valid information about how things bring about changes. With such knowledge an individual can use his or her resources to intervene in the course of events. In addition, one must have knowledge of (1) *Price*—what one must give up in order to

secure a thing; (2) *Priority*—deciding which is more important among options of harm or benefit; and (3) *Duty*—the concept which concerns the quality of life for the larger society. Thus an individual may receive reduced benefit, but the total result is gain.[7] Under point three is introduced what we designate as *moral duties*—those limitations which we impose upon ourselves to confer equal benefits on all concerned. Thus we arrive at guidelines for the group which we designate as norms. The function of such norms is to provide guidance for those who are trying to answer questions about what someone might do. Clearly knowing the value of something is relevant when people want to know what they *should* do. In the activities section we have included a guidelines sheet for analyzing decisions in terms of values.

In summary, then, we have sought to demonstrate how one can measure the capacity of some sort of circumstance or event to make a favorable difference in people's lives. The addition of the moral dimension to this conception of clue analysis can result from an inquiry into the underlying values which guide the decision-making process.

Inquiry into Future Values

If one uses the model of the inquiry process normally utilized in the social studies, it involves five components. These are:

1. The delineation of a problem. Here the word "problem" is broadly conceived to include any event, circumstance, etc. as described in the previous sections on value analysis.

2. The formulation of alternative hypotheses, with hypotheses defined as tentative courses of action on proposed solutions.

3. The process of seeking new knowledge or information relevant to the problem. This is not unlike the process of seeking knowledge of benefits or negative effects presented earlier.

4. Making decisions as to specific courses of action or policies—in effect, which, if any, of the hypotheses (#2) are probable.

5. Taking action in accord with the dictates of reason as formulated in previous parts.

To this point, this inquiry process, while not being value free, has not necessarily produced reflection on the values implicit in the process. This inquiry into values comes through the addition of the next component presented in the form of questions.

6. What values are involved when the alternative hypotheses were formed?

What underlying values about the problem, the issues, etc. influenced the shaping of the hypothesis?

What do they show about conceptions of the nature of humankind, society, reality?

What are one's responsibilities to the larger society?

And for the added dimension of the future, two additional components can be:

7. What are the underlying assumptions about the future? Is there an assumption that the future will be like the past? How do assumptions about the future shape decisions in the present? Are assumptions about the future consistent and/or compatible with probable realities?

8. What changes or modifications in values and value structures must be made in the future? Which present values promise utility for the future and should be retained? The addition of components six, seven, and eight thus transform an inquiry process into a future values endeavor that can be highly cognitive.

Changing Images of Humankind: The Transformational Ethic

One of the problems of teaching in the area of values is the difficulty of achieving consensus on just which values should guide such endeavors. The problem is perhaps even more pronounced when one considers the future because it ne-

cessitates reflection upon what sort of society one prefers. On pages 12–13 we
provided a sketch of the work of Willis
Harman, in which he suggests that we are
approaching one of the great transformations of human history. Whether or not
this transformation will occur, of course,
we cannot know. Regardless of whether it
does or not, the characteristics of an adequate image of humankind presented by
Harman can provide useful ideas for
values for the future.

The following characteristics of a new
image for humankind are a provisional list
resulting from Stanford Research Institute's analysis of contemporary social
problems, studies of plausible alternative
futures, and consideration of society's
dominant image of humankind.

A Holistic Sense of Perspective

A holistic perspective and understanding of life seems absolutely vital if we are
to overcome the fragmentation and alienation that have become so common in the
latter part of the industrial era.

Ecological Ethic

An ecological ethic is necessary if [hu-
man beings are] to avoid destroying the
complex life support system on which our
continued existence on the planet depends. It must involve not only a sense of
mutual self-interest between individuals,
but also the interests of fellow men [and
women] and the more extensive interests
among fellow creatures (both near and
far, both present and future).

Self-Realization Ethic

. . . the proper end of all individual experience is the evolutionary and harmoni-
ous development of the emergent self
(both as a person and as a part of wide
collectivities), and that the appropriate
function of social institutions is to create
an environment which will foster that
process.

Multi-dimensional,
Multi-faceted, and Integrative

. . . If a new image is to contribute to
resolution of the planet's woes, it must
provide for an integrative reconciliation of
the apparent dichotomies between op-
posing images . . . it must build on past
successful images . . . it has to be absorbed into the lives of the people and the
institutions of society without the dis-
ruptions that accompany most revolutions
. . . [it] must somehow be made compatible with the basic symbols of the American experiment . . . .

Balancing and Coordinating
Satisfactions Along Many Dimensions

. . . to provide a needed corrective to
the one-sided life style of achieving an increased standard of living that has accompanied the growth of the value-empty
economics and science of our industrial
society. . . . Such a new image . . . might
be supportive of a philosophy (and indeed a public strategy) of "well-being"
. . . [it] should lead to understandings of
personal and social actions suitable for
the highly interconnected and complex—
but limited—environment that the symbol
"spaceship earth" has come to signify.

Experimental and Open-ended

Self-consciously evolutionary rather
than dogmatic and paradigm-bound attitudes and images are necessary. It is un-
reasonable to expect the rate of change
in society to diminish. If the society of the
future is to avoid the image obsolescence
and crisis that our present society faces, it
will be necessary to anticipate—rather
than just react to—the necessity for such
paradigm changes, and continuously to
seek more adequate conceptions and images.[8]

CLASSROOM IMPLEMENTATION OF VALUE ANALYSIS

In the pages which follow are a number of specific suggestions for introducing the value dimension into the classroom. Since virtually every futures topic has a values component, the problem is to decide just when, how, and for what purpose the value dimension is approached.

In order to assess change, it is useful to begin the study with some device to determine student attitudes and values on the issue under consideration prior to studying it. Numerous futures questionnaires, opinionnaires, inventories, and pre-test instruments can be found in the references cited in chapter 7. For practical purposes and to make the choices more in accord with the particular design of the course or unit, the teacher will likely prefer to construct his/her own instrument. Ordinarily these devices provide a statement as to some possible future condition or state of affairs and then ask the student to respond by stating whether the condition will happen, when it will happen, how he/she would likely feel about it (i.e., would approve, disapprove, or not care), and to provide reasons why.

TECHNOLOGICAL DEVELOPMENTS WHICH MAY OCCUR IN THE FUTURE

Development	I think it (check one)		If it did occur, I:		Reasons for choice
	will occur	won't occur	would like it	wouldn't like it	
Ability to pre-determine and choose sex of unborn children	____	____	____	____	_____
Home education by computers and video discs	____	____	____	____	_____
Use of chemicals to aid learning and memory	____	____	____	____	_____
Replacement of worn out or malfunctioning body parts (mechanically or by substitution)	____	____	____	____	_____

(Note: Such lists can be extended to suit the needs of the area under consideration. For most effective use, the developments, events, etc. should be appropriately categorized. Some may be technological; others may relate to social changes, such as marriages and life style or global issues. A close perusal of the stated unit or course objectives will suggest the type for inclusion.)

Below is an "Options for the Future"
preference inventory based on current trends and alternatives.

OPTIONS FOR THE FUTURE

Instructions: In the column at the left are some current trends. In the column at the right is listed an alternative to the trend. Select the option you prefer by checking the column. If you prefer some other alternative, write it in the space provided.

_____ Continued, unrestricted industrial economic growth

_____ Growth planned in terms of the quality of human life.

Other alternative:

_____ Continued and increasing use of non-renewable energy sources.

_____ Energy conservation and restrictions on energy consumption.

Other alternative:

_____ Continued use and expansion of technology wherever possible.

_____ Assessment and evaluation of technological growth in terms of its impact on the quality of human life.

Other alternative:

_____ Increased urbanization and centralization of population.

_____ Dispersal of population and movements to rural environments.

Other alternative:

_____ Unrestricted exploitation of the environment.

_____ Environmental impact, concerns, and issues predominate.

Other alternative:

_____ Growth of more sophisticated and powerful weapons systems.

_____ Arms limitation and disarmament.

Other alternative:

_____ Growth of large multinational corporations and conglomerates.

_____ Smaller production units with international trade agreements.

Other alternative:

_____ Expanded growth of influence of a technical class of people.

_____ Public participation in technical decisions.

Other alternative:

———— Impersonal institutions and individual alienation from society.

———— Revived emphasis on the human
dimensions of society.

Other alternative:

———— Materialism and competitive self-
interest as individual motivation.

———— Life styles based on simplicity and
cooperation.

Other alternative:

———— Orientation toward a consumer society with status based on consumption.

———— Production and use of what is
needed for living.

Other alternative:

———— Built-in obsolescence and "latest"
styles, models, etc. receiving emphasis.

———— Goods that last and/or are easily
repaired. Serviceability is empha-
sized.

Other alternative:

———— Individual identity achieved through
conformity to demands of groups,
cultures, or nations.

———— Self identified by self-development
of one's human potential and identification with human kind.

Other alternative:

QUESTIONS OF VALUE ANALYSIS FOR MAKING RATIONAL CHOICES

1. How does the outcome of (proposed action) benefit some individual, group, or institution?

2. Why, how, or in what way is the outcome of (proposed action) preferable to some other mode of conduct or end state of existence?

3. Is (proposed action) of benefit to me at the expense of some other individual, group, or institution?

4. What is the net gain of (proposed action) to all concerned?

5. What are the positive and negative factors which must be weighed?

6. What do I value that affects how I assess this action?

7. Is the likely resultant condition or state of affairs beneficial in the future as well as in present?

8. Are there likely to be unanticipated effects which may result?

9. Can I defend this proposed action as a moral act?

On the following page is a sheet for analyzing decisions in terms of values. An analytical tool such as this provides a means for evaluating the quality of particular decisions in terms of the criteria proposed. Thus a teacher can render a judgment about the end result as well as the means utilized in the process. Importantly, such analyses make the process explicit to the student.

ANALYZING DECISIONS IN TERMS OF VALUES

Value object: Issue, problem, set of circumstances, which require a decision as to action.

MAJOR CONSIDERATIONS

Decision to take a specific action
Action:

_____

_____

How will this action produce change?

_____

_____

Anticipated results
Immediate future

_____

_____

Meliorative Claims

_____

_____

Near future

_____

_____

Price

_____

_____

_____

Distant future

_____

_____

Priority

_____

_____

_____

What is the benefit?

_____

_____

Duty

_____

_____

Who benefits?

_____

FINAL DECISION
Follow original choice _____
Modify choice _____
Reasons for modifying_____

Possible unanticipated results

_____

_____

_____

_____

_____

VALUE CHANGE ACTIVITY

Have students select some characteristic value; e.g., material acquisitiveness—the acquiring of "things" which presumably make our lives easier and add to our social status, such as a new car (two or three new cars), a large home, etc.

Ask:
1. Where did we get this value?
2. How do you suppose this value became a part of our culture?
3. What does this value do for us? What purpose does it serve? Are these things good for us? bad for us? or neutral?
4. Does this value still function in our present-day society as it did historically?
5. If you have this value, could you change it?
6. Why might you want to change it?
7. Would your changing of this value have any effect on other people?
8. What if the majority of the people changed their minds on this value? What would be the effect?

VALUES DISCUSSION ACTIVITY

1. Make a list of the values which you think characterize our present-day society.
2. If you think the value still serves a useful purpose in our society, put a plus (+) beside it. If you think it does *not* serve a useful purpose, put a negative (−) beside it. If you feel it is neutral, put an asterisk (*) beside it. Write a sentence or two justifying your rating.
3. How do you think your parents would rate this value? Is your rating different? If so, how would you account for the change?
4. Do you think this value will still be a good one in the future (a specific date could be given)? Why or why not?
5. If you think this value will not be useful in the future, how can it be changed? What should replace it?
6. Create an alternative value for the future which will better serve the needs of humankind. In relation to this value; describe the conditions which you feel should prevail in the future and how these conditions might be created.

FUTURIST'S DILEMMA ACTIVITY

An activity which can produce student reflection on the conflict between short-term personal "good" and the longer-range social "good" is a variation of the prisoner's dilemma. In the prisoner's dilemma two individuals are charged with the same crime. The prosecuting attorney tells each that the one who confesses will receive a shorter sentence, but the one who does not confess will receive a harsh sentence. If both confess, then they will each receive some intermediate sentence between the two extremes. The situation is presented below:

Prisoner 1 options	Prisoner 2 options	
	Not Confess	Confess
Not confess	3 years each	10 years for 1 and 6 months for 2
Confess	6 months for 1 and 10 years for 2	5 years each

In this activity students put themselves in the position of each prisoner and go through the reasoning of each. In each instance the student is placed in the position of comparing his/her personal "good" (avoidance of a long sentence) against the possible action of another individual's "good."

The same dilemma can be applied to the individual *vis à vis* the total society by the use of issues, problems, and circumstances related to the future through use of a variation of a cross-impact matrix. The same issue can then be expanded to a consideration of the possible conflicts between national self-interest and global interests by projecting issues, problems, and/or proposed policies into a similar form. Obviously, there are usually more than two alternative courses of action. The point of this dilemma exercise is to have students consider social arrangements which will induce people to give up short-run individual benefits for the sake of longer-run collective areas from which the individuals also benefit. Ecological, environmental, and war-peace issues are particularly suited for this activity. On the following page is a schema for using this activity in class.

SOCIETY
(collective individuals)

	Effect on Individual (if only individual action)	Effect on Society (if *all* took the *same* action)
Action Choice A		
Alternative Action Choice B		
Alternative Action Choice C, etc.		

INDIVIDUAL

GLOBAL SOCIETY
(collective nations)

	Effect on Nation (if only nation took action)	Effect on Global Society (If *all* took the *same* action)
Action Choice A		
Alternative Action Choice B, etc.		

NATIONAL SOCIETY
(Individual Nation)

NOTES

[1]Robert L. Heilbroner, *An Inquiry Into the Human Prospect* (New York: W. W. Norton & Co. Inc., 1974), p. 22.

[2]Fred Newmann and Donald W. Oliver, *Clarifying Public Controversy* (Boston: Little, Brown & Company, 1970). James P. Shaver and Harold Berlak, editors, *Democracy, Pluralism, and the Social Studies* (Boston: Houghton Mifflin Company, 1968). James P. Shaver and William Strong, *Facing Value Decisions* (Belmont, California: Wadsworth Publishing Company, Inc., 1976). Also see Lawrence E. Metcalf, editor, *Values Education* (Washington D.C.: National Council for the Social Studies, 41st Yearbook, 1971).

[3]Sidney B. Simon and Howard Kirschenbaum, editors, *Readings in Value Clarification* (Minneapolis: Winston Press, Inc., 1973). Sidney B. Simon, Leland W. Howe, and Howard Kirschenbaum, *Values Clarification* (New York: Hart Publishing Company, 1972). Merrill Harmin, Howard Kirschenbaum, and Sidney B. Simon, *Clarifying Values Through Subject Matter* (Minneapolis: Winston Press Inc., 1973).

[4]Kurt Baier and Nicholas Rescher, editors, *Values and the Future* (New York: The Free Press, 1969), p. 5. Our treatment of the analysis of the concept of value comes basically from Part One of this work.

[5]Milton Rokeach, *The Nature of Human Values* (New York: The Free Press, 1973), p. 5. Also see: Milton Rokeach, *Beliefs, Attitudes, and Values* (San Francisco: Jossey-Bass Inc. Publishers, 1972).

[6]Baier and Rescher, *Values and the Future*, p. 47.

[7]*Ibid.*, p. 51.

[8]Stanford Research Institute, *Changing Images of Man*, Policy Research Report 4 (Menlo Park, California), May, 1974, pps. 143–156. Also see Willis Harman, *An Incomplete Guide to the Future* (San Francisco: San Francisco Book Co., 1976).

5.
Images of the Future Through Science Fiction

The uses of science fiction in education have already been explored in many books and articles. This brief chapter will attempt to summarize some of the basic notions about this form of literature and to suggest some specific applications to teaching about the future, together with some starting points and potential resources.

The maturing of science fiction as a meaningful and an increasingly respectable branch of literature in many ways parallels the emergence of futurism as a legitimate field of inquiry. Science fiction (hereinafter designated as SF) has, in fact, come to be recognized as a form of writing whose study is indispensable to the study of the future.

It is also true, however, that SF has had a low reputation among scholars and literary critics—particularly among those for whom this form of writing is composed primarily of stories of adventure and romance set against backgrounds of space travel, gadgetry, and/or contact with sentient beings from other worlds.

This image of SF remains partially true; but many recent stories have transcended the simplistic themes, plots, and other shortcomings of earlier works. It is a fact that since its emergence as a literary form in the pulp magazines of the 1920s, SF has been disproportionately preoccupied with "space-opera" plots, journeys to other (usually inhabited) worlds, and gadgets such as ray guns, time machines, and robots. Over the years, however, the predictable plots, "thin" and stereotyped characters, and third-rate writing have yielded more and more to works

of artistic merit and soaring imagination. The themes of SF have reached out to cover an amazing variety of subjects and future possibilities. Plots have become more sophisticated, complex, and subtle, often with deep allegorical meanings. Style and scientific plausibility have also improved markedly.

Defining the nature of SF is a matter of interpretation, and since there are many different interpretations of this genre, there are several possible definitions. Definition is also made difficult because of the fact that there have been several different "waves" of SF writing over the years, each with its distinctive characteristics. A major rift exists, for example, between "mainstream" SF, which traces its roots to the romance and adventure stories of the 1920s, and the so-called second "new wave" SF, which is oriented toward social criticism and experimentalism.

This second category, which includes what Robert A. Heinlein calls "Realistic Future-Scene Fiction,"[1] will be the focus of this chapter. While we do not wish to denigrate those works which exist purely for entertainment, our purpose here is to assist teachers to understand the relationships between SF and studying the future and to help them identify the types of SF which can be the most useful in teaching about the future.

In defining this genre, we must first state that the belief that SF is about science is somewhat misleading. Although many SF stories are set in the future with backgrounds containing social and technological innovations which do not exist

To take a step into the future we need to shift our weight to the opposite foot.

—William Irwin Thompson

today, the "science" usually serves only as the setting in which the action takes place, and only rarely becomes a major focal point. Many stories have little or no science in them at all, but instead portray alternate realities, extraterrestrial life, or improbable settings.

The following represent some of the varied definitions of SF:

"Thus science fiction is predominantly a speculative literature in which the reader is invited to ponder in some detail the effect that a given advance, change, discovery, or technological breakthrough might have upon society as we know it and upon human beings as we know them."[2]

"SF is a prose narrative that deals with a situation that could not happen in the world as we know it, but deals with it so that it appears scientifically plausible and realistic."[3]

"Science fiction: fiction based on rational speculation regarding the human experience of science and its resultant technologies."[4]

"Science fiction is that class of prose narrative treating of a situation that could not arise in the world as we know it, but which is hypothesized on the basis of some innovation in science or technology, or pseudo-science or pseudo-technology, whether human or extraterrestrial in origin."[5]

"Science fiction is neither science nor fiction but man in search of himself and the meaning of his existence."[6]

SF is often an attempt to predict possible futures. Through SF we are exposed to a vast range of possibilities and po-

tentialities. This characteristic suggests that an alternate name for this type of literature might be more appropriate. Possibility fiction, speculative fiction, and social science fiction are three names which have been suggested. But to avoid confusion we will continue to use the term science fiction.

The writers of "good" SF, all of whom are highly creative individuals, attempt to introduce their readers to imaginative explorations of what may lie over the horizon, or they may invent a situation which is closer to pure fantasy simply to speculate or raise important questions about such topics as the interface between people and technology, the next possible stage of human evolution, alternative belief or value systems, possible alternate realities, or the possibility of life forms on other worlds.

Like science itself, SF is an accumulation of discoveries. It feeds upon itself by building and improving on earlier ideas, continuously striving to transform itself with novel and more imaginative forms, breaking taboos and other barriers as it strikes out in new directions. Thus, unlike other types of literature, SF constantly renews and regenerates itself from within as well as keeping ahead of scientific and societal developments. The acceleration of change in society mandates a corresponding response in SF writing. Trips to the moon are passé; even the eventual establishment of a colony on' the moon has become too mundane a topic about which to write. But stories about ecology, pollution, overpopulation, genetic manipulation, nuclear war, and rampant technology, which carry these themes to some future conclusion, are still topical. The startling fact about stories based on these themes, however, is that many of them were written long before they became acute societal problems, demonstrating the anticipatory character of SF writing. To be shocked and surprised by SF is to be better prepared for tomorrow.

As we have mentioned earlier, present actions will determine the shape of the future. Negative scenarios in SF writings may serve as an early warning system to help societies avoid actions which may have negative consequences. The classic negative SF scenario of our times, George Orwell's *1984,* may or may not have had an effect in actually delaying or retarding the growth of government surveillance. Few modern works of fiction have had the societal impact of *Uncle Tom's Cabin* or Upton Sinclair's *The Jungle,* but the possibility of a work of SF having such an effect is not unlikely, since SF is basically social criticism.

Another important fact about SF which must be mentioned here is that this genre generally focuses on the advancement of ideas, rather than on the development of characters. Such stories generally explore human responses to novel circumstances, raising questions about how we may react to similar situations. The protagonists are made to deal with conditions with which we have not yet been confronted, as SF stories attempt to supply tentative answers to such provocative questions as: How might people react during the aftermath of a nuclear war or a plague which decimates 95 percent of the population? How will human beings behave as colonists in space? What might happen should we encounter aliens from another world more advanced than ours? The answers provided in works of SF supply clues in the continuing search for guiding values, for an understanding of human behavior, and for comprehension of the nature of the universe. Ultimately,

these are questions with which futurism is also concerned.

Relating SF to Teaching About The Future

For purposes of relating SF to the study and teaching of the future, we will focus here on five major themes:

1. Science fiction is a form of social criticism. It is uniquely suited to identifying the weaknesses of society by carrying certain tendencies or trends to what might appear to be their logical conclusions. By providing detailed portraits or scenarios of future societies, it identifies, often quite vividly, the consequences to which present conditions may lead. The roots of these future societies can invariably be found in the present because of the inability of even the most imaginative SF writers to fully transcend the cultural perspectives from which they write. Thus a society choked and poisoned by pollution, as portrayed in John Brunner's *The Sheep Look Up,* is inexorably pulled further toward disaster as the people refuse to recognize that they themselves are collectively responsible for their condition. The dystopias (anti-utopias) portrayed in many SF novels reflect a basically pessimistic view of human nature. Naturally, the use of such negative scenarios in the classroom should be balanced with those which portray more optimistic futures.

2. Closely related to the first theme is the use of SF to facilitate the exploration of beliefs and values, and the possible consequences to which they may lead. Alternative value systems portrayed in many SF stories raise serious questions concerning our adherence to such instrumental values as materialism, the exploitation and conquest of nature, the competitive work ethic, faith in technology, and individualism. Such stories ask us to reflect upon the possible effects on the future of our continued adherence to certain values, and occasionally confront us with sit-

uations in which value systems radically different from our own are posited. Such is the case in Robert A. Heinlein's *Stranger in a Strange Land,* whose main protagonist, having been born of human parents but raised on Mars, returns to Earth bringing with him the values of the Martian culture in which he was raised, and gradually gains the loyalty of a following who see him as a Christ-like figure.

A multitude of moral and ethical questions are raised by stories which deal with such topics as human evolution, cloning, time travel, new technologies, immortality, and so on. Reflection upon such issues may enable students to make wiser choices for the future.

3. Quite obviously, SF can act as a stimulus to thinking about the future in more imaginative and creative ways. It can help establish new directions, new orientations, and new patterns in students' thinking processes. SF contains an endless variety of possibilities to suggest new models of reality. There are descriptive and analytical elements in SF, but the stories tend mostly to be provocative by creating new hypotheses which allow us to look at things in new ways. Hyperbole, satire, allegory, distorted images—the effect of SF is to create new juxtapositions of ideas which may facilitate the invention of new patterns of thinking and the rejection of old ones.

The idea that we need new perspectives and new solutions to our societal problems is becoming increasingly accepted. SF helps to create new frames of reference through which conditions may begin to be perceived in significantly different ways. While we do not claim that the reading of SF will substantially alter the direction of societal trends, students systematically exposed to new ideas through such literature will probably begin to think differently about the things we take for granted or accept unquestioningly.

4. SF is also a rich storehouse of ideas

about alternative futures. The sheer number of SF stories provides an endless variety of conceptions regarding alternate societies, alternate cultures, and alternate values. Among its many features, SF illustrates the contrasts between the present and an imagined future.

By tapping the resources of SF, students are exposed to a virtually unlimited form of brainstorming. From a fixed frame of reference and a limited view of reality, students will encounter shocking assumptions, outrageous postulates, and startling propositions in the novels and short stories of SF.

5. Finally, SF can be useful in preparing students for a world of accelerating change. We surprise ourselves now by reading SF, and thus possibly avoid the shock of being caught unaware by a surprising turn of events. The unique and alien worlds portrayed in many SF stories may give students a feeling of uneasiness, sadness, or revulsion; but such feelings may help to prepare them psychologically for the future. At the very least, having been exposed to such a variety of scenarios as is contained in SF, they may begin to feel somewhat less uncomfortable with new ideas, and somewhat less startled by unusual developments.

Resources

In the remainder of this chapter we will attempt to identify selected works of SF that represent certain themes or ideas which might be suitable for use in teaching about the future.

There are obvious differences between SF novels and short stories. Novels permit a more complete development of a theme or idea, allowing the protagonists, and sometimes even their decendants, to live through the events or situations in which they find themselves. Through the novel, the SF writer can provide sufficient detail to create more convincing settings and to describe more completely alien worlds, strange cultures, or alternate value systems. On the negative side, however, novels often contain complexities of plot, detail, and character development which, in a futures course, might involve needless distractions or misappropriations of classroom time. On the other hand, many novels contain a combination of topics and themes which can be woven into two or more units. One example of this is in Arthur C. Clarke's *Imperial Earth,* which deals with politics and government, space colonization, cloning, and advanced technology. Another use for the SF novel is in an individualized reading program within a futures course.

Short stories are naturally more adaptable to one or two class periods. They are written in a more sparse and more economical prose and get to the point much more quickly than the novel. Usually there is just one main theme in a SF short story, fast-paced action, and little character development. There are several excellent anthologies of SF short stories which are primarily concerned with realistic-scene fiction in near- to medium-term future settings.

The following resources are intended to be used as starting points. First of all, it would be helpful to obtain some of the standard works of SF history and criticism, sources of annotated bibliographies, and teacher's guides. Some examples of these are the following:

History and Criticism—Reginald Bretnor, ed., *Science Fiction, Today and Tomorrow.* Baltimore: Penguin Books, 1974; Robert Scholes and Eric S. Rabkin, *Science Fiction: History—Science—Vision.* Oxford: Oxford University Press, 1977; Alexi and Cory Panshin, *SF in Dimension.* Chicago: Advent Publishers, 1976; L. David Allen, *Science Fiction Reader's Guide.* Lincoln, Nebraska: Centennial Press, 1974; Brian Ash, ed., *The Visual Encyclopedia of Science Fiction.* New York: Harmony Books, 1977; Sam J. Lundwall, *Science Fiction: What It's All About.* New York: Ace Books, 1971; Brian Ash, *Faces of the Future: The Lessons of Science Fiction.* New York: Taplinger Publishing Company, 1975.

Annotated Bibliography—Neil Barron, *Anatomy of Wonder: Science Fiction* (New York: R. R. Bowker Company, 1976).

Teacher's Guides—L. David Allen, *The Ballantine Teachers' Guide to Science Fiction.* New York: Ballantine Books, 1975; Elizabeth Calkins and Barry McGhan, *Teaching Tomorrow: A Handbook of Science Fiction for Teachers.* Dayton, Ohio: Pflaum/Standard, 1972; Bernard C. Hollister and Deane C. Thompson, *Grokking the Future: Science Fiction in the Classroom.* Dayton, Ohio: Pflaum/Standard, 1973; Suzanne Millies, *Science Fiction Primer for Teachers.* Dayton, Ohio: Pflaum/Standard, 1975.

Science Fiction Anthologies

There are scores of SF anthologies in print, including several series which reprint the best stories each year. Perhaps the most ready access to realistic future-scene SF can be had in thematic anthologies, of which the following are representative:

Allen, Dick and Allen, Lori, eds. *Looking Ahead: The Vision of Science Fiction.* New York: Harcourt, Brace, Jovanovich, Inc., 1975.

Allen, Dick, ed. *Science Fiction: The Future.* New York: Harcourt, Brace, Jovanovich, Inc., 1971.

Asimov, Isaac. *Nine Tomorrows: Tales of the Near Future.* Greenwich, Conn.: Fawcett Crest, 1959.

Clem, Ralph; Greenberg, Martin Harry; and Olander, Joseph, Eds. *The City 2000 A.D.: Urban Life Through Science Fiction.* Greenwich, Conn.: Fawcett Crest, 1976.

Dann, Jack and Dozios, Gardner, eds. *Future Power: A Science Fiction Anthology.* New York: Random House, 1976.

Disch, Thomas M., ed. *The Ruins of Earth.* London: Arrow Books Ltd., 1973.

Edelstein, Scott. *Future Pastimes.* Nashville, Tenn.: Aurora Publishers, Inc., 1977.

Elwood, Roger, ed. *Future City.* New York: Pocket Books, 1973.

———, ed. *The Other Side of Tomorrow.* New York: Pyramid Books, 1973.

———, ed. *Tomorrow's Alternatives.* New York: Collier Books, 1973.

Hollister, Bernard, ed. *Another Tomorrow.* Dayton, Ohio: Pflaum Publishing, 1974.

Hoskins, Robert, ed. *The Future Now: Saving Tomorrow.* New York: Fawcett Crest, 1977.

———, ed. *The Liberated Future: Voyages into Tomorrow.* New York: Fawcett Crest, 1974.

Greenberg, Martin Harry and Warrick, Patricia S., eds. *Political Science Fiction: An Introductory Reader.* Englewood Cliffs, New Jersey: Prentice-Hall, Inc., 1974.

———; Milstead, John W.; Olander, Joseph D.; and Warrick, Patricia, eds. *Social Problems Through*

Science Fiction. New York: St. Martin's Press, 1975.

Harrison, Harry, ed. *The Year 2000: An Anthology.* New York: Berkley Publishing Corporation, 1970.

Heinlein, Robert A. *The Past Through Tomorrow: Future History Stories.* New York: Berkley Publishing Corporation, 1975.

Katz, Harvey A.: Warrick, Patricia; and Greenberg, Martin Harry, eds. *Introductory Psychology Through Science Fiction.* Chicago: Rand McNally College Publishing Company, 1974.

Mason, Carol; Greenberg, Martin Harry; and Warrick, Patricia, eds. *Anthropology Through Science Fiction.* New York: St. Martin's Press, 1974.

McNelly, Willis E. and Stover, Leon E., eds. *Above the Human Landscape: An Anthology of Social Science Fiction.* Pacific Palisades, Calif.: Goodyear Publishing Company, Inc., 1972.

Milstead, John W.; Greenberg, Martin Harry; Olander, Joseph D.; and Warrick, Patricia, eds. *Sociology Through Science Fiction.* New York: St. Martin's Press, 1974.

Ofshe, Richard, ed., *The Sociology of the Possible.* Englewood Cliffs, New Jersey: Prentice-Hall, Inc., 1970.

Olander, Joseph; Greenberg, Martin Harry; and Warrick, Patricia, eds. *American Government Through Science Fiction.* Chicago: Rand McNally College Publishing Company, 1974.

Roselle, Daniel, ed. *Transformations: Understanding World History Through Science Fiction.* Greenwich, Conn.: Fawcett Publications, Inc., 1973.

_____, ed. *Transformations II: Understanding American History Through Science Fiction.* Greenwich, Conn.: Fawcett Publications, Inc., 1974.

Sargent, Pamela, ed. *Bio-Futures: Science Fiction Stories About Biological Metamorphosis.* New York: Vintage Books, 1976.

Scortia, Thomas N. and Zebrowski, G., eds. *Human-Machines: An Anthology of Stories About Cyborgs.* New York: Vintage Books, 1975.

Schwartz, Sheila, ed. *Earth in Transit: Science Fiction and Contemporary Problems.* New York: Dell Publishing Co., Inc., 1976.

Silverberg, Robert, ed. *Windows into Tomorrow.* New York: Pinnacle Books, 1974.

Science Fiction Novels and Short Stories Illustrating Specific Futures Themes

The following list includes a few of the more well known and critically acclaimed works which we have classified into fourteen topical categories. Some works deal with several themes, and we have entered some titles in more than one category. Also, since some works are available through more than one publisher, we have not included information about the publishers.

New Belief Systems, New Religions: Roger Zelazny, *Lord of Light;* Robert A. Heinlein, *Stranger in a Strange Land;* Walter M. Miller, Jr. *A Canticle for Leibowitz.*

Biological Engineering: Kate Wilhelm, *Where Late the Sweet Birds Sang;* Pamela Sargent, *Cloned Lives;* Ben Bova, *The Multiple Man;* Arthur C. Clarke, *Imperial Earth.*

Cities, Urban Problems: Robert Silverberg, *The World Inside;* Isaac Asimov, *The Caves of Steel;* Clifford D. Simak, *City;* James Blish, *Cities in Flight.*

Doom and Cataclysm: J. G. Ballard, *The Drought, The Drowned World, The Wind from Nowhere;* Brian Aldiss, *The Long Afternoon of Earth;* Pat Frank, *Alas, Babylon;* George Stewart, *Earth Abides;* Philip K. Dick, *Dr. Bloodmoney;* Larry Niven and Jerry Pournelle, *Lucifer's Hammer;* Fritz Leiber, *The Wanderer;* John Brunner, *The Sheep Look Up.*

Ecology and Pollution: Frank Herbert, *Dune, The Green Brain;* Ursula LeGuin, *The Word for World Is Forest;* John Brunner, *The Sheep Look Up.*

Human Evolution/Expanded Human Abilities: Arthur C. Clarke, *Childhood's End;* Theodore Sturgeon, *More Than Human;* Clifford D. Simak, *Time and Again;* Frederick Pohl, *Man Plus.*

Mind Control and Drug Use: Stanislaw Lem, *The Futurological Congress;* Aldous Huxley, *Island;* Daniel Keyes, *Flowers for Algernon;* Philip K. Dick, *A Scanner Darkly;* Michael Crichton, *The Terminal Man.*

Politics and Government: Frank Herbert, *Dune;* George Orwell, *1984;* Isaac Asimov, *Foundation Trilogy;* Clifford D. Simak, *Way Station;* Robert A. Heinlein, *Have Space Suit, Will Travel.*

Population: Lester del Rey, *The Eleventh Commandment;* Harry Harrison, *Make Room! Make Room!;* J. G. Ballard, *Billennium;* Philip K. Dick, *Do Androids Dream of Electric Sheep?;* Frederick Pohl and C. M. Kornbluth. *The Space Merchants.*

Race Relations, Prejudice: Peter Dickinson, *The Green Gene;* Olaf Stapledon, *Odd John;* John Wyndam, *Rebirth, The Midwich Cuckoos;* Pierre Boulle, *Planet of the Apes.*

Space Exploration and Colonization: Ray Bradbury, *The Martian Chronicles;* Larry Niven, *Ringworld;* Arthur C. Clarke, *Rendezvous with Rama, 2001: A Space Odyssey, The City and the Stars, Imperial Earth;* Ben Bova, *Millennium.*

Technology and Computers: Harlan Ellison, *I Have No Mouth, and I Must Scream*; D. F. Jones, *Colossus*; Ira Levin, *This Perfect Day*; Kurt Vonnegut, Jr., *Player Piano*; John Brunner, *The Shockwave Rider*.

Utopias and Dystopias: Mack Reynolds, *Looking Backward from the Year 2000*; B. F. Skinner, *Walden II*; Ursula LeGuin, *The Dispossessed*; Robert Silverberg, *The World Inside*; Kurt Vonnegut, Jr., *Player Piano*; Eugene Zamiatin, *We*.

War, Revolution, Militarism: Robert A. Heinlein, *The Moon Is a Harsh Mistress, Starship Troopers, Revolt in 2100*; Walter A. Miller, Jr., *A Canticle for Leibowitz*; Nevil Shute, *On the Beach*; E. A. Van Voght, *The Weapon Shops of Isher*.

NOTES

[1]Alexi and Cory Panshin, *SF in Dimension* (Chicago: Advent Publishers, 1976), p. 9.

[2]Alan E. Nourse, "Science Fiction and Man's Adaptation to Change," in Reginald Bretnor, ed., *Science Fiction Today and Tomorrow* (Baltimore: Penguin Books Inc., 1974), p. 122.

[3]Suzanne Millies, *Science Fiction Primer for Teachers* (Dayton, Ohio: Pflaum Publishing, 1975), p. 1.

[4]Reginald Bretnor, "Science Fiction in the Age of Space," in Reginald Bretnor, ed., *Science Fiction Today and Tomorrow*, p. 150.

[5]Kingsley Amis, "Starting Points," in Dick Allen, ed., *Science Fiction: The Future* (New York: Harcourt, Brace, Jovanovich, Inc., 1971), p. 247.

[6]Aaron W. Hillman, *Speculative Fiction: Trips into Inner and Outer Space* (Santa Barbara, Calif.: Confluent Education Development and Research Center), p. i.

6.
Evaluating the Outcomes of Futures Education

The Larger Problem of Evaluation: The Humanistic Alternative

Futures education brings to the schools an opportunity to make substantial changes in the educational process. Aside from introducing a new perspective in both content and methodology, futures education offers a humanistic conception of the teaching-learning process that seeks to provide a positive environment for learning. The area of evaluation and measurement is frequently the part of the teaching-learning process that undermines or even destroys the effectiveness of the educational efforts that have preceded it. Prior to considering specifics of evaluation in futures education, it will be helpful to note that we will advocate a broad program of evaluation which will include objective measurement devices as well as other evaluational procedures. Therefore it is appropriate to make a distinction between evaluation and measurement. Here we will use the term *evaluation* to indicate all methods of obtaining information relevant to the attainment of objectives, and *measurement* will be restricted to methods of obtaining information by externally objective measures such as tests. Thus, evaluation includes measurement but is not restricted to "objective" type measures. Evaluation is thus broader and can include more subjective measures, such as check lists, opinionnaires, as well as teacher judgment. This distinction is especially important to keep in mind because assessing the outcomes of futures education necessitates the use of a wide range of evidence-gathering techniques.

In traditional conceptions of the educational process, evaluation and measurement are culminating activities utilized by teachers for the purpose of assessing student achievement and assigning a grade. At the end of the unit of study the student takes a test and receives a score and/or grade which shows how the student stands relative to his/her peers. At that point, regardless of the amount of knowledge or skills the student possesses or what he/she understands about the subject studied, the class proceeds to the study of a new topic. If a given student's measured level of achievement is judged to be "D" or "F," that student, too, proceeds to the new unit, though with the admonition to "do better on the next test."

The effect of the judgmental processes in the school is one of the subjects addressed by Benjamin Bloom in *Human Characteristics and School Learning.*[1] Bloom points out that the student is judged more frequently during his/her school career than at any other time in life. Further, the student is judged on relative, rather than on absolute norms. From these judgments made by others and her/his own judgments, the student forms her/his perceptions of adequacy and inadequacy to deal with further learning. As Bloom puts it, "The system of grading and instruction operates to open doors for some students while effectively closing doors for others."[2] The pernicious results of these procedures, however, is not restricted to the school years. The future effect is even greater.

Today, as never before, we have the opportunity to take hold of our destiny. We are at last free for the task of growing up as a species. But growing up is not comfortable; it is accompanied by stresses and strains.

L. S. Stavrianos

Even more important is the effect of the student's school-related affect on his willingness to learn in his post-school years. The Unesco report, *Learning to Be,* holds that in modern societies further learning throughout life is a major adaptive mechanism for dealing with change—whether the change be in the area of work or in the larger developments in the society. Negative attitudes toward school and school learning have serious consequences for the individual's use of further learning as an adaptive method of dealing with his own problems as an adult as well as in part determining his life-style and response to societal changes.[3]

These postulates of Bloom, while relevant to the whole educational process, are crucial to futurism—an area of study predicated upon increasing the capacity of students to cope with change and to imagine future alternatives. Should the evaluational procedures utilized in futures units or courses continue to stress competition and relative norms, they would tend to work against the accomplishment of many futures objectives.

Special Problems of Evaluating Futures Education

As we have noted, futures education is a complex interplay of cognitive and affective dimensions with added intuitive and moral aspects. As such, the evaluation of futures education presents one of the more thorny problems in dealing with futurism in the classroom. As noted by Stock, "One of the weaknesses in present future studies programs . . . is the lack of adequate methods for determining the extent to which such programs have met their stated goals."[4]

At a time in education when accountability and "back to the basics" are guiding principles, should futures education not be able to point to educationally defensible and measurable outcomes it is doubtful that it will have much success in gaining space in the social studies curriculum. From an analysis of numerous future studies courses and units, it appears that the problem of assessing outcomes is related in large measure to the lack of clarity and specificity of the objectives of futures education.[5]

Possibly because of the nebulous nature of the future and because so many futures objectives have an implicit values orientation, the measurement of the outcomes of future studies is more troublesome. Adding to and complicating the problem of measurement of outcomes is the humanistic orientation of futures teachers, which often includes an anti-testing bias. For these reasons and because of our own commitment to a more humane educational process, we will advocate evaluation procedures which we believe can assess outcomes without producing the negative effects cited by Bloom.

Why Evaluate? A Rationale

The answer one gives to this question has a significant effect upon how one approaches all dimensions of the teaching-learning process, as well as upon how one assesses learning. Too frequently the answer given is "to be able to assign grades." The realities of schooling necessitate that such an answer be retained among the reasons we evaluate, but it is the least important reason. A more basic reason is to determine the extent to which previously agreed upon objectives are being accomplished. A corollary of this reason is to assist in diagnosing the problems and difficulties students are encountering in the learning process and to be able to prescribe remedial learning activities. This view of evaluation provides information about the level of student learning as well as about our effectiveness in teaching. Thus our conception of evaluation for futures education is broad and includes all methods of obtaining information relevant to the attainment of objectives.

We have previously defined effective teaching as teaching which accomplishes its objectives. It is thus axiomatic that evaluation is performed on the basis of the stated objectives. Whether one chooses to go to the extent of stating behavioral objectives is a personal decision, but in any case the objective should be unambiguous and specific enough to guide instructional efforts as well as to suggest a logical means of measuring the outcomes. In any case, the first step towards effective evaluation comes from the formulation of a clearly stated, specific objective.

The second task of the evaluator is to analyze the stated objective and to determine whether the sought outcome is basically cognitive (involving knowledge and/or skills) or affective (involving attitudes, beliefs, values). Once the objective is properly classified, the next task is to ask oneself what would provide suitable evidence that the student possesses the knowledge or skill or has dealt with the attitude or value.

The above procedures should be carried out prior to any teaching if they are to be of any value in the teaching-learning process. Thus, students should know the unit objectives prior to instruction, as well as the type and quantity of specific evidence which will be accepted to indicate that the knowledge or skill is possessed or that the attitude or skill has been dealt with. The idea is, quite simply, to make evaluation an ongoing part of the teaching-learning process and to remove the "guessing game" from evaluation. Such procedures should be strategically incorporated into the unit plans as a means of checking on progress toward unit objectives. Thus we are presenting the case for non-competitive mastery level learning as the basis for evaluation in futures studies units and courses.

Here is an illustration of the foregoing as it might occur in a classroom situation:

Course Objective (7.0 from Appendix—Guidelines for the Determination of Objectives)
    I. The student should demonstrate an understanding of the ideas of major futurists.

Unit Objectives
    IA. The student will demonstrate knowledge of Willis Harman's theory of the coming transformation.
    IB. The student will demonstrate knowledge of Daniel Bell's conception of post-industrial society.
    IC. The student will be able to make a general statement relating Harman's transformational theory to Bell's concept of post-industrial society.

Daily Objectives
    IA1. Given a list of twelve factors in our present industrial era world, the student will select those factors which are illustrative of how the industrial era paradigm is no longer viable.
    IB2. In an essay of no more than two hundred words the student will describe at least five characteristics of post-industrial society.
    IC3. After reading two articles, one describing Harman's transformational theory and one describing Bell's notion of post-industrial society, the student will relate the two articles by producing a general statement such as "the post-industrial society necessitates a new image of humankind."

Course Objective (2.0 from Guidelines for the Determination of Objectives)
II. The student should understand the concept of change.

Unit Objectives
IIA. The student should understand some of the various ways in which change occurs.
IIB. The student should understand the possible effects of change on personal goals and aspirations.

Daily Objectives
IIA1. Given a reading on the introduction of the wheel to the Papago Indians around 1900, the student will form three hypotheses as to the ways in which Papago life changed as a result of the wheel.
IIB2. After interpreting statistical data on energy resources and the depletion of fossil fuels, the student will hypothesize upon likely modes of transportation in the future and how these will affect family structure.

Evaluating
High Cognitive Domain Outcomes

As we have seen, the cognitive domain consists of both knowledge and the manipulation of that knowledge which we call intellectual skills and abilities. Futurism relies upon combining knowledge of the social sciences, sciences, history, philosophy, and virtually every segment of human endeavor. While the cognitive area of futurism is amenable to assessment through many of the conventional means of measurement utilized in social studies classes, the particular characteristics of futurism afford opportunities to extend our repertoire of measurements by utilizing the methodological tools of futurists.

The unique perspective of futurism is that the various areas of knowledge are utilized selectively in such a way as to allow the futurist to go beyond the knowledge so assembled to *tentative* new insights. This is an adapted definition of discovery learning. The word *tentative* is necessary here to indicate that the verification of new insights will usually require the passage of time. Nevertheless, in classroom application this perspective offers unique teaching and evaluation opportunities.

Thus futurism presents special opportunities to utilize analysis, synthesis, and evaluation, the highest levels of the cognitive domain. A word of caution is in order at this point, however, since our society is biased in favor of analysis while often punishing equally necessary attempts at synthesis. Further caution is in order, too, since taxonomy and method can become the enemy of thought. Still, with these reservations in mind, let us proceed to offer specific suggestions for the evaluation of futurism objectives.

Tests

Teacher-constructed objective tests can be utilized to measure student knowledge of facts, concepts, and generalizations. Aside from low-level factual knowledge, test items should seek to achieve the application of knowledge in a new situation. Item forms may be multiple choice, matching, key-list, or short answer.

Essay tests offer opportunities for students to demonstrate knowledge of relationships as well as the evaluation of such skills as hypothesis formation and other inquiry skills. Students may be asked to analyze reading passages for the main idea or be asked to synthesize several passages into a new communication.

It is hardly necessary for us to caution that all such tests of the above type should conform to the requirements for good classroom tests. It is beyond the scope of this Bulletin to deal with this area in detail. Numerous references on testing are available. We have listed two basic references in our footnotes.[6]

Our only further note before proceeding to suggest other means for evaluation is to caution the prospective practitioner to keep in mind the admonitions of Benjamin

Bloom regarding the potentially harmful effects of traditional conceptions of evaluation.

Other Evaluational Techniques

While testing can measure certain dimensions of student learning, futures education affords a wide variety of other evaluational techniques. The focus in this area is both on the knowledge to be learned and the manipulation of that data in thinking. Student projects and activities of various types can be devised to have the student become familiar with the methodologies used by futurists. Thus students can construct their own futures wheels, relevance trees, cross-impact matrices, trends, and projections. They can conduct their own surveys, polls, and opinionnaires. They can plot graphs and construct charts which depict data relevant to future inquiries. The reader may wish to refer back to some of these techniques as presented on pages 34, 35, 36. Such projects can be evaluated for the quality, consistency, and logic of thought presented. Consistency between data and outcomes or conclusions are especially to be noted. The important thing for the teacher using such projects for evaluation is that the student be made aware of the criteria which will be used in evaluation. Also important for the teacher is the diagnostic value of such projects. By analyzing student projects the teacher can identify deficiencies and direct the student accordingly. A total evaluational program in futures education will rely heavily upon a wide range of individual written work as well as participation in group projects.

Scenario and science fiction writing can be evaluated in terms of how imagination, creativity, knowledge, and skill influence the final product. Questions which may be used to evaluate such efforts are:

Does the student consider all pertinent variables?

Does the student account for the rela-tionships which exist?

Does the student anticipate and demonstrate how the variables interact?

What are the inconsistencies?

How creative is the product?

Does it demonstrate novel and/or unanticipated dimensions?

Assessing Affective Domain Outcomes

While the cognitive domain outcomes can be evaluated rather precisely, the affective outcomes are more difficult. Yet it has been stressed that in many ways futurism is an attitude. In Chapter 4 we presented a conception of value which makes it easier for the teacher to deal with values and the future from a more practical perspective. In this we stress a value-object analysis approach which focuses upon rational decision-making.

In evaluation in this area it is important to note that an affective objective contains or is based upon implicit cognitive elements. As we have sought to demonstrate in our discussion of values, there is a cognitive base in the value area and, to the extent an individual has relevant information (whether he/she likes the implications of the information or not), he/she can make more rational decisions.

The crucial factor in teaching becomes the communication to the student that decisions can be rational or irrational and that attitudes and values which we hold can either promote or inhibit rational decision-making. If the student is in possession of the relevant information on a given issue or problem, he/she must realize that while he/she may choose to act contrary to the dictates of that information, undesirable consequences may result and the decision must be classified as irrational.

An excellent source for dealing with the change-decisions-consequences approach which we have advocated in our chapter on values is the Forty-Seventh Yearbook of the National Council for the Social Studies, edited by Dana G. Kurfman, and entitled *Developing Decision-*

Making Skills. In particular, the chapter on evaluation by Celeste P. Woodley and Laura A. Driscoll presents "A Model and Suggestions for Evaluating Decision-Making Skills." While the overall focus is on cognitive skills, part II of their decision-making skills schema focuses upon:

II. **Recognizing the Values Implicit in a Decision Situation**
   A. *Cognitive Task:* Inferring
   B. *Object of the Cognitive Task:* Values and/or value conflicts implicit in a decision situation.
   C. *Prior Conditions Necessary for the Demonstration of the Skill:* Must know the meaning of "value" and "value conflict"; must know what the differences are between facts and values; must have had practice with inferring.
   D. *Criteria Against Which To Test Products or Behavior Which Demonstrate Skill:*
      1. The items named as values must be logically derived from the decision occasion; that is, must plausibly attach to goals or means alternatives, to persons making or affected by the coming decision;
      2. The items named as values must qualify as values; that is, as central beliefs about how one ought or ought not to behave, or about some end-state of existence, worth or not worth attaining.

The naming of the values and/or the identification of real or potential value-conflicts must be more than wild guesses. To show inferencing, the student must be able to associate the value with the characteristics of the situation or person(s) in the situation that suggested it.[7]

Evaluating value decisions can be accomplished through a variety of paper and pencil techniques as well as by teacher observation. A number of futures questionnaires and opinionnaires have been devised which provide opportunities for assessing change between pre- and post-instructions. Examples of these have been provided in the chapter on values.

Evaluation and Futures Education: Concluding Observations

We have sought to demonstrate that evaluation is an ongoing process that is an integral part of the teaching-learning process. We have shown how futurism lends itself especially well to this approach. Forecasting methodologies represent procedures which are, in effect, evaluation as they are utilized. While the end result of a forecast—the projected condition—cannot immediately be ascertained, the proper application of the technique can be assessed. Student projects, papers, and classwork should be evaluated, commented upon, and returned. Points can be awarded accordingly and utilized as part of the student's grade. Yes, much more record-keeping will be required; but evaluation which is incorporated into the teaching-learning process and which the student comes to view as part of that process loses much of its threatening, inhibiting nature for the student.

NOTES

[1]Benjamin S. Bloom, *Human Characteristics and School Learning* (New York, McGraw-Hill, 1976).

[2]Benjamin S. Bloom, "Affective Outcomes of School Learning," *Phi Delta Kappan,* Vol. 59, November 1977, No. 3, p. 195.

[3]*Ibid.,* p. 196.

[4]Richard B. Stock, "Future Studies in U.S. High Schools—Part II," *World Future Society Bulletin,* Vol. XI, No. 4, July-August, 1977, p. 14.

[5]Cordell M. Svengalis, *The Implications of Futures Education for Secondary School Social Studies,* unpublished Ph.D. dissertation (Iowa City: University of Iowa, 1978).

[6]For a treatment of the area, see: Harry D. Berg, editor, *Evaluation in Social Studies* (Washington, D.C.: 35th Yearbook of the National Council for the Social Studies, 1965). See also: Benjamin Bloom, J. Thomas Hastings, and George Madaus, *Handbook on Formative and Summative Evaluation of Student Learning* (New York: McGraw-Hill, 1971).

[7]Celeste P. Woodley and Laura A. Driscoll in *Developing Decision-Making Skills,* Dana G. Kurfman, editor. (Washington, D.C.: 47th Yearbook of the National Council for the Social Studies, 1977).

7.
Resources for Teaching About the Future

Resources for the study of the future are voluminous, and guides to teaching about the future are becoming increasingly available. While we recognize the formidable task involved in becoming familiar with several new fields of study, we wish, nevertheless, to provide the means to do so. We have divided the following bibliography into several categories in order to facilitate the search for materials under different headings.

A. Books Suitable for Student Texts

Carpenter, Jack. *Destination Tomorrow*. W. C. Brown, 1972.

Dunstan, Maryjane and Garlan, Patricia W. *Worlds in the Making: Probes for Students of the Future*. Prentice-Hall, 1970.

_____. *Star Sight: Visions of the Future*. Prentice-Hall, 1977.

Farrell, Edmund J. *Science Fiction/Science Fact*. Scott Foresman, 1974.

Goodykoontz, William F. *The Future: Can We Shape It?* Scholastic, 1973.

Hellfach, Judith. *The Future of the Environment*. Prentice-Hall, 1977.

_____. *The Future of the Family*. Prentice-Hall, 1977.

_____. *The Future of the Government*. Prentice-Hall, 1977.

_____. *The Future of Work*. Prentice-Hall, 1977.

Leinwand, Gerald, *The Future*. Pocket Books, 1976.

Moffitt, Donald, Ed. *The Wall Street Journal Views America Tomorrow*. Dow Jones, 1977.

Theobald, Robert. *Futures Conditional*. Bobbs-Merrill, 1972.

B. The Basic List

Clarke, Arthur C. *Profiles of the Future*. Revised edition. Popular Library, 1977. A non-technical, science-oriented inquiry into possible alternative futures. Suitable for high school students. A mind-stretching classic. (pb)*

_____
*Indicates whether a book may be obtained in paperback (pb), or only in hard cover (hc).

Cornish, Edward. *The Study of the Future*. The World Future Society, 1977. A comprehensive introduction to futurism, with brief treatments of several topics. Does not go into great depth. Surveys many basic ideas and concepts, and contains an annotated bibliography. (pb)

Falk, Richard. *This Endangered Planet: Prospects and Proposals for Human Survival*. Vintage Books, 1972. A comprehensive primer on the relationships between ecological concerns and world politics. Develops a basic rationale for the design of a model for world order. (pb)

Harman, Willis W. *An Incomplete Guide to the Future*. San Francisco Book Company, 1976. Suggests a coming transformation and discusses the role of futures thinking in restructuring society. Deals with the coming shift away from the industrial-era paradigm and toward a trans-industrial paradigm based on a humanistic-ecological ethic. A very thought-provoking book. (pb)

Miles, Rufus. *Awakening from the American Dream—The Social and Political Limits to Growth*. Universe Books, 1976. Deals with the overstrained capacity of human beings to conceive, design, manage, support, and adapt to increasingly complex systems of human interdependence. Suggests a turn toward a more moderate energy civilization and proposes a number of fascinating social and political alternatives. (pb)

Murray, Bruce. *Navigating the Future*. Harper & Row, 1975. Sees a coming "crunch" brought about by continued population growth and dwindling resources. He warns that we are in the midst of the most rapid and significant change in history; and he proposes a number of suggestions to get us out of the situation we are in. He sees the future as far from being hopeless, but fraught with dangers. (hc)

Spekke, Andrew. *The Next 25 Years: Crisis and Opportunity*. World Future Society, 1975. This is an anthology of readings based on sessions held at the Second General Assembly of the World Future Society in 1975. There are forty-three selections arranged in ten thematic sections ranging from world community, to intimate relationships, to forecasting. Many of the top futurists are represented. (pb)

The trouble with our time is that the future is not what it used to be.

—Paul Valery

Schumacher, E. F. *Small Is Beautiful: Economics As If People Mattered.* Harper & Row, 1973. Revolutionary thinking about an alternative to large technology, which the author refers to as "intermediate technology." This book has become a "bible" to an increasing number of individuals who seek alternatives to the dehumanizing, exploitive, polluting way of life brought about by industrialization. Another classic in futurist thought. (pb)

Thompson, William Irwin. *Darkness and Scattered Light.* Anchor Doubleday, 1978. This latest of the author's four future-oriented books is perhaps his best. He sees the world entering an age of chaos prior to the emergence of a planetary renaissance, one of the primary characteristics of which he calls the "meta-industrial village." (pb)

Tugwell, Franklin. *Search for Alternatives.* Winthrop Publishers, 1973. An excellent anthology containing some of the best shorter pieces of futurist writing. Among the ones included are John Platt's "What We Must Do," and Elise Boulding's "Futurology and the Imaging Capacity of the West." (pb)

C. Highly Recommended for More Advanced Reading

Baier, Kurt and Resher, Nicholas, eds. *Values and the Future.* The Free Press, 1969. Even though several years old, this book remains a useful handbook devoted to the exploration of the possible impact of values upon society in the future. (pb)

Brown, Lester. *The Twenty-Ninth Day.* W. W. Norton & Company, 1978. This book explores the basic dilemma of exponential growth of the population and its projected effects on the carrying capacity of the earth and its resources. This is an in-depth exploration of the biological systems on which humanity depends, and how their interaction, together with the projected energy shortages, will bring about a profound change that will affect virtually every facet of human existence in the next few decades. (pb)

Commoner, Barry. *The Closing Circle: Nature, Man & Technology.* Bantam Books, 1971. One of the best early books devoted to exploring the relationships between industrialism and the ecological system. Much information basic to an understanding of ecology. (pb)

Dickson, Paul. *The Future File.* Rawson Associates, 1977. A general handbook on futurism, written in a popular style, with a wealth of information. (hc)

Feinberg, Gerald. *Consequences of Growth.* Seabury Press, 1977. Provocative, profound discussion of the social implications and ramifications of several possibilities for the future, including space colonization, control over aging, long-range goals and environmental problems, etc. (hc)

Ferkiss, Victor. *The Future of Technological Civilization.* George Braziller, 1974. A very detailed and profound analysis of the political philosophy (liberalism) which, from the author's perspective, has gotten us into the predicaments we presently face. A better future, the author believes, can be obtained not by attacking problems piecemeal but by considering some rather thorough changes in the structure and philosophy of our political-economic system. (hc)

Fromm, Erich. *To Have or To Be.* Harper & Row, 1976. This is not a futurist book *per se,* but its philosophy has profound implications for the future. Basically, the author condemns the radical hedonism and materialism of the modern era, and suggests that a possible solution to many of our problems lies in a transformation of consciousness toward a more altruistic level of being, sharing, and giving. A challenging philosophy for the future, and an excellent book. (hc)

Heilbroner, Robert. *An Inquiry into the Human Prospect.* W. W. Norton, 1974. Raises the basic question: Is there hope for human beings? The author says we are suffering from a crisis of self-confidence and from an awareness that the quality of life is deteriorating. He discusses, pessimistically, the problems of overpopulation, environmental decay, etc. He sees increasing tensions in the years ahead, and suggests that we are too short-sighted to be able to meet effectively the challenges we face. (pb)

Henderson, Hazel. *Creating Alternative Futures: The End of Economics.* Berkeley Publishing Corp., 1978. A provocative collection of the author's articles on several economically related topics, dealing with such issues as economic growth, inflation, technology assessment, and the emerging "counter-economy." (pb)

Jungk, Robert. *The Everyman Project.* Liveright, 1977. Very informative introduction to the many ways in which individuals may become involved in creating alternative futures. This is basically a book on how to democratize the future by getting the ordinary citizen involved. (hc)

Kahn, Herman. *The Next 200 Years.* William Morrow, 1976. The author is a technological optimist. He believes that the so-called doomsday thinkers are wrong in predicting catastrophe. Though we may have a few minor setbacks, he says that populations and economies will continue to grow far into the future, and that this growth will be sustainable and beneficial. Should be read to balance the more pessimistic accounts of the future. (pb)

McHale, John. *The Future of the Future.* George Braziller, 1969. A wide-ranging overview, aided by scores of charts and photographs, with particular emphasis on ecology, technology, and planetary resources. (pb)

Meadows, Donella, et al. *The Limits to Growth.* Signet, 1972. Controversial report, based on a computerized model, that suggests that the convergence of population growth, resource depletion, pollution, etc. will soon lead to disaster unless we quickly change our ways. Many subsequent books refer to the conclusions in this study, so it should be read for basic background. (pb)

Slater, Philip. *The Pursuit of Loneliness.* Beacon Press (2nd edition), 1976. Incisive sociological critique of contemporary American culture. The author analyzes what he believes is wrong with our society and suggests some challenging alternatives. Challenging reading, and well worth the effort. (pb)

Stavrianos, L. S. *The Promise of the Coming Dark Age.* W. H. Freeman, 1976. An optimistic view of the future taken in the light of historical perspective. Looks at the seeming chaos as not only the death agonies of the old order, but the birth pangs of a new golden age. (pb)

Theobald, Robert. *Beyond Despair.* New Republic Book Company, 1976. Analysis of several of our contemporary problems. The author, who has written several other future-oriented books, believes that part of the solution lies in creating a new system of understandings among people. He assumes that people can learn to modify their destructive behaviors if they can be made to realize that it is in their own best interests to do so. A very plausible theory, clearly argued. (pb)

D. General

Beitz, Charles and Washbum, Michael. *Creating the Future: A Guide to Living and Working for Social Change.* Bantam, 1974.

Bell, Daniel. *The Coming of Post-Industrial Society.* Basic Books, 1973.

Boulding, Kenneth. *The Meaning of the Twentieth Century.* Harper & Row, 1964.

Bundy, Robert, ed. *Images of the Future.* Prometheus Books, 1976.

de Jouvenel, Bertrand. *The Art of Conjecture.* Basic Books, 1967.

Esfandiary, F. M. *Optimism One.* Popular Library, 1970.

_____. *Telespheres.* Popular Library, 1977.

_____. *UpWingers.* Popular Library, 1973.

Fabun, Don. *The Dimensions of Change.* Glenco Press, 1971.

_____. *The Dynamics of Change.* Prentice-Hall, 1967.

Feinberg, Gerald. *The Prometheus Project: Mankind's Search for Long-Range Goals.* Doubleday, 1968.

Ferkiss, Victor. *Technological Man.* Mentor Books, 1969.

Ferre, Frederick. *Shaping the Future: Resources for the Post-Modern World.* Harper & Row, 1976.

Jungk, Robert and Galtung, Johan. *Mankind 2000.* London: Allen and Unwin, 1969.

Kostelanetz, Richard, Ed. *The Edge of Adaptation.* Prentice-Hall, 1973.

_____. *Human Alternatives.* Morrow, 1971.

_____. *Social Speculations.* Morrow, 1971.

Kuhn, Thomas S. *The Structure of Scientific Revolutions.* Phoenix Books, second edition, University of Chicago Press, 1970.

Marien, Michael. *Societal Directions and Alternatives.* Information for Policy Design, 1976.

McHale, John. *The Changing Information Environment.* Westview Press, 1976.

_____. *World Facts and Trends.* Collier, 1972.

Platt, John. *The Step To Man.* Wiley, 1966.

Polak, Fred. *The Image of the Future.* Oceana Publications, 1961.

_____. *Prognostics.* Elsevier, 1971.

Slater, Philip. *Earthwalk.* Bantam, 1974.

Theobald, Robert. *An Alternative Future for America's Third Century.* Swallow Press, 1976.

Thompson, William Irwin. *At the Edge of History.* Harper & Row, 1971.

Toffler, Alvin. *Future Shock.* Random House, 1970.

_____. *The Futurists.* Random House, 1972.

_____. *The Eco-Spasm Report.* Bantam, 1975.

Vacca, Roberto. *The Coming Dark Age.* Doubleday, 1973.

World Future Society. *The Future: A Guide to Information Sources.* World Future Society, 1977.

E. Creativity

Biondi, Angelo. *The Creative Process*. D.O.K. Publishers, 1972.

_____. *Have An Affair With Your Mind*. Creative Synergetic Associates, 1974.

DeBono, Edward. *Lateral Thinking*. Ward Lock, 1970

_____. *New Think*. Basic Books, 1968.

_____. *Teaching Thinking*. Temple Smith, 1976.

Parnes, Sidney J. *Aha!: Insights Into Creative Behavior*. D.O.K. 1975.

_____. *Creativity: Unlocking the Human Potential*. D.O.K., 1972.

_____. *Toward Supersanity*. D.O.K., 1973.

F. Energy, Environment, and Resources

Brown, Lester. *By Bread Alone*. Praeger, 1974.

Brown, William and Kahn, Herman. *Let There Be Energy*. Crowell, 1978.

Brubaker, Sterling. *In Command of Tomorrow: Resource and Environmental Strategies for Americans*. Johns Hopkins University Press, 1975.

Clark, Wilson. *Energy for Survival*. Anchor Books, 1975.

Commoner, Barry. *The Poverty of Power*. Bantam, 1976.

Ehrlich, Paul and Pirages, Dennis. *Ark II: Social Response to Environmental Imperatives*. Viking, 1974.

Ehrlich, Paul. *The End of Affluence*. Ballantine, 1974.

Fuller, Buckminster. *Operating Manual for Spaceship Earth*. Simon & Schuster, 1970.

Goodavage, Joseph. *Our Threatened Planet*. Simon & Schuster, 1978.

Hardin, Garrett. *Exploring New Ethics for Survival*. Penguin, 1968.

_____. *The Limits of Altruism*. Indiana University Press, 1977.

Hayes, Dennis. *Rays of Hope*. W. W. Norton, 1977.

Kenward, Michael. *Potential Energy*. Cambridge University Press, 1976.

McHale, John. *The Ecological Context*. George Braziller, 1969.

Mesarovic, Mihajio and Pestel, Eduard. *Mankind at the Turning Point*. Signet, 1974.

Nash, Hugh, ed. *Progress As If Survival Mattered*. Friends of the Earth, Inc., 1977.

Ophuls, William. *Ecology and the Politics of Scarcity*. Freemen, 1977.

Perelman, Lewis. *The Global Mind: Beyond the Limits to Growth*. Mason/Charter, 1976.

Sansom, Robert. *The New American Dream Machine: Toward a Simpler Lifestyle in an Environmental Age*. Doubleday, 1976.

Schneider, Stephen. *The Genesis Strategy: Climate and Global Survival*. Plenum, 1976.

Theobald, Robert. *Habit and Habitat: A Call for Fundamental Changes to Solve the Environmental Crisis*. Prentice-Hall, 1972.

G. Economics and Work

Barnet, Richard and Muller, Ronald E. *Global Reach: The Power of the Multinational Corporations*. Simon and Schuster, 1974.

Best, Fred. *The Future of Work*. Prentice-Hall, 1973.

Daley, Herman. *Toward a Steady-State Economy*. W. H. Freeman, 1973.

Dunnette, Marvin. *Work and Nonwork in the Year 2001*. Brooks/Cole, 1973.

Heilbroner, Robert. *Business Civilization in Decline*. Harper & Row, 1975.

Toffler, Alvin. *The Eco-Spasm Report*. Bantam, 1975.

Watt, Kenneth. *The Titanic Effect*. Sinauer, 1974.

H. Education

Brameld, Theodore. *The Teacher as World Citizen*. ETC, 1976.

Ciba Foundation Symposium. *The Future as an Academic Discipline*. Elsevier, 1975.

Conrad, David. *Education for Transformation: Implications in Lewis Mumford's Ecohumanism*. ETC, 1976.

Hack, Walter. *Educational Futurism—1985*. McCutchan, 1971.

Hostrop, Richard, ed. *Education–Beyond Tomorrow*. ETC, 1975.

_____. *Foundations of Futurology in Education*. ETC, 1973.

Kauffman, Draper L., Jr. *Futurism and Future Studies*. NEA, 1976.

_____. *Teaching the Future*. ETC, 1976.

Muller, Herbert. *The Uses of the Future*. Indiana University Press, 1974.

Postman, Neil and Weingartner, Charles. *Teaching as a Subversive Activity*. Dell, 1969.

Reischauer, Edwin O. *Toward the 21st Century: Education for a Changing World*. Vintage, 1973.

Rubin, Louis, ed. *The Future of Education*. Allyn and Bacon, 1975.

_____. *Educational Reform for a Changing Society*. Allyn and Bacon, 1978.

Shane, Harold. *Curriculum Change Toward the 21st Century*. NEA, 1977.

_____. *The Educational Significance of the Future*. Phi Delta Kappa, 1973.

Toffler, Alvin, ed. *Learning for Tomorrow: The Role of the Future in Education*. Random House, 1974.

I. Life Styles and Changing Sex Roles

Bernard, Jessie. *The Future of Marriage*. Bantam, 1972.

Francoeur, Robert T. and Francoeur, Anna. *Eve's New Rib: Twenty Faces of Sex, Marriage, and Family*. Delta, 1973.

_____. *The Future of Sexual Relations*. Prentice-Hall, 1974.

_____. *Utopian Motherhood: New Trends in Human Reproduction*. A. S. Barnes, 1973.

Libby, Roger, and Whitehurst, Robert N. *Marriage and Alternatives*. Scott, Foresman and Company, 1977.

Otto, Herbert. *The Family in Search of a Future*. Appleton-Century-Crofts, 1970.

_____. *Love Today: A New Exploration*. Association Press, 1972.

Pawley, Martin. *The Private Future: Causes and Consequences of Community Collapse in the West*. Random House, 1974.

Ramey, James. *Intimate Friendships*. Prentice-Hall, 1976.

Smith, James R. and Smith, Lynn G. *Beyond Monogamy: Recent Studies of Sexual Alternatives in Marriage*. Johns Hopkins University Press, 1974.

Tripp, Maggie. *Woman in the Year 2000*. Dell, 1974.

J. Alternative Realities

Jonas, Doris and Jonas, David. *Other Senses, Other Worlds*. Stein and Day, 1976.

LeShan, Lawrence. *Alternate Realities*. Ballantine, 1976.

_____. *The Medium, The Mystic and the Physicist*. Ballantine, 1974.

Maruyama, Magorah and Harkins, Arthur, eds. *Cultures Beyond Earth, The Role of Anthropology in Outer Space*. Vintage, 1975.

Mitchell, Edgar. *Psychic Exploration*. G. P. Putnam, 1974.

Pearce, Joseph Chilton. *The Crack in the Cosmic Egg*. Pocket Books, 1971.

_____. *Exploring the Crack in the Cosmic Egg*. Pocket Books, 1974.

Roszak, Torodore. *Unfinished Animal*. Harper & Row, 1976.

Slater, Philip. *The Wayward Gate: Science and the Supernatural*. Beacon Press, 1977.

Tart, Charles. *Altered States of Consciousness*. Doubleday, 1972.

Velikovsky, Immanuel. *Worlds in Collision*. Dell, 1950.

_____. *Earth in Upheaval*. Pocket Books, 1977.

White, John and Kripner, Stanley. *Future Science: Life Energies and the Physics of Paranormal Phenomena*. Anchor Books, 1977.

K. Politics and Government

Bezold, Clement, ed. *Anticipatory Democracy: People in the Politics of the Future*. Vintage Books, 1978.

Michael, Donald. *On Learning to Plan—and Planning to Learn*. Jossey-Bass, 1973.

Perloff, Harvey, ed. *The Future of the U.S. Government*. Braziller, 1971.

Waskow, Arthur. *Running Riot*. Herder and Herder, 1970.

Lakey, George. *Strategy for a Living Revolution*. W. H. Freeman, 1973.

L. Technology

Berry, Adrian. *The Next Ten Thousand Years*. Mentor, 1975.

Cross, Nigel, et al. *Man-made Futures: Readings in Society, Technology and Design*. Hutchinson Educational, 1974.

Ferkiss, Victor. *Technological Man*. Mentor, 1969.

Gendron, Bernard. *Technology and the Human Condition*. St. Martin's Press, 1977.

Hellman, Hal. *The City in the World of the Future*. Evans, 1970.

_____. *Communications in the World of the Future*. Evans, 1975.

_____. *Technophobia: Getting Out of the Technology Trap*. Evans, 1976.

_____. *Transportation in the World of the Future*.

Martin, James and Norman, Adrian. *The Computerized Society*. Prentice-Hall, 1970.

Moore, Wilbert. *Technology and Social Change*. Quadrangle, 1972.

Muller, Herbert. *The Children of Frankenstein*. Indiana, 1972.

Mumford, Lewis. *The Myth of the Machine: The Pentagon of Power*. Harcourt, 1970.

Rosen, Stephen. *Future Facts*. Simon and Schuster, 1976.

Stine, G. Harry. *The Third Industrial Revolution*. Putnam, 1975.

Teich, Albert, ed. *Technology and Man's Future*. St. Martin's, 1972.

M. Simple Living and Decentralization in a Technological Age

Borsodi, Ralph. *This Ugly Civilization*. Simon and Schuster, 1929.

Callenbach, Ernest. *Living Poor with Style*. Bantam, 1972.

Fritsch, Albert, et al. *99 Ways to a Simpler Lifestyle*. Center for Science in the Public Interest, 1976.

Gorney, Roderick. *The Human Agenda*. Bantam, 1973.

Greely, Andrew M. *No Bigger Than Necessary*. NAM, 1977.

Illich, Ivan. *Tools for Conviviality*. Harper & Row, 1973.

Lakey, George. *Strategy for a Living Revolution*. Grossman, 1973.

Simple Living Collective. *Taking Charge: Personal and Political Change Through Simple Living*. Bantam, 1977.

Roszak, Theodore. *Where the Wasteland Ends: Politics and Transcendence in Postindustrial Society*. Doubleday, 1972.

Taylor, Gordon Rattray. *Re-Think: A Paraprimitive Solution*. E. P. Dutton, 1973.

N. Society and Culture

Etzioni, Amitai. *The Active Society*. Free Press, 1968.

Fromm, Erich. *The Revolution of Hope: Toward a Humanized Technology*. Bantam, 1968.

Hall, Edward T. *Beyond Culture*. Anchor Press, 1976.

Lundborg, Louis. *Future Without Shock*. W. W. Norton, 1974.

Mead, Margaret. *Culture and Commitment*. Doubleday, 1970.

Tucille, Jerome. *Who's Afraid of 1984?* Arlington House, 1975.

Roszak, Theodore, *Person/Planet*. Doubleday, 1978.

Wagar, Warren W. *The City of Man*. Houghton Mifflin, 1973.

O. Transformation and Transcendence

De Chardin, Pierre Teilhard. *The Future of Man*. Harper & Row, 1964.

_____. *Toward the Future*. Harcourt, 1973.

Fromm, Erich. *The Well-Being of Man and Society*. Seabury Press, 1978.

Hunter, Robert. *The Storming of the Mind*. Anchor, 1972.

Jantsch, Erich. *Design for Evolution*. Braziller, 1975.

Land, George T. *Grow or Die*. Dell, 1973.

Leonard, George. *The Transformation*. Delacorte, 1972.

_____. *The Silent Pulse,* 1979.

Mumford, Lewis. *Transformations of Man*. Harper & Row, 1964.

Reiser, Oliver. *Cosmic Humanism*. Schenkman, 1966.

Salk, Jonas. *Survival of the Wisest*. Harper & Row, 1973.

Thompson, William Irwin, ed. *Earth's Answer*. Harper & Row, 1977.

_____. *Passages About Earth*. Harper & Row, 1974.

P. International Relations and World Order

Brown, Lester. *World Without Borders*. Vintage, 1973.

Falk, Richard A. *A Study of Future Worlds*. Free Press, 1975.

Kothari, Rajni. *Footsteps into the Future*. Free Press, 1974.

Laszlo, Ervin, et al. *Goals for Mankind*. E. P. Dutton, 1977.

Thorbeke, William J. *Mankind at the Crossroads*. Oceana, 1975.

Tinbergen, Jan, ed. *RIO: Reshaping the International Order*. E. P. Dutton, 1977.

Q. Biomedical and Psychological

Chavkin, Samuel. *Psychosurgery and Mind Control*. Houghton Mifflin, 1978.

Etzioni, Amitai. *Genetic Fix*. Macmillan, 1973.

Howard, Ted and Rifkin, Jeremy. *Who Should Play God?* Dell, 1977.

Loye, David. *The Knowable Future*. John Wiley and Sons, 1978.

Packard, Vance. *The People Shapers*. Little Brown, 1977.

Pines, Maya. *The Brain Changers*. Signet, 1973.

Restak, Richard. *Pre-Meditated Man: Bioethics and the Control of Future Human Life*. Viking, 1975.

Schrag, Peter. *Mind Control*. Pantheon Books, 1978.

Segerberg, Osborn Jr. *The Immortality Factor*. Bantam, 1974.

Taylor, Gordon R. *The Biological Time Bomb*. New American Library, 1968.

R. Population and Food

Brown, Lester. *By Bread Alone*. Praeger, 1974.

Ford, Barbara. *Future Food: Alternate Protein for the Year 2000*. William Morrow, 1978.

Parsons, Jack. *Population vs. Liberty*. Prometheus, 1973.

Spengler, Joseph. *Population and America's Future*. Freeman, 1975.

S. Multimedia Kits on the Future

Forecasting the Future: Can We Make Tomorrow Work? Harper & Row

Projections for the Future: A Humanist Model. Crystal Productions, P.O. Box 11480, Aspen, Colorado 81611

The Future. Scholastic Literature Filmstrips

Americans' Changing Lifestyles. Current Affairs

2000 A.D. Newsweek

Change Here for Tomorrow. Doubleday Multimedia #73202

Dynamics of Change. Doubleday Multimedia #74302

Toward the Year 2000: Can We Survive the Future? The Center for the Humanities, Inc. #258

An Inquiry Into the Future of Mankind: Designing Tomorrow Today. The Center for Humanities, Inc. #258

The New Genetics: Rights and Responsibilities. The Center for Humanities, Inc. #1002

Free Will and Utopias. Schloat

Human Values in an Age of Technology. The Center for the Humanities, Inc. #222

The Future of the Family. Guidance Associates

Changing Role of Women. Scott Educational Division

Science Fiction. Center for Humanities, Inc.

T. Games and Simulations

Global Futures Game. Earthrise, Inc. Box 120 Annex Station, Providence, Rhode Island 02901

Futuribles. World Future Society Book Service

Future Decisions. The I.Q. Game. SAGA Publications, RR 2 Greentree Road, Lebanon, Ohio 45036

Future Shock. World Future Society Book Service

Futures Planning Games. Greenhaven Press

Cope. Interact

New Town. World Future Society Book Service

Utopia. Interact

Humanus. Simile II

Futura City. Newsweek Educational Division

U. Periodicals

Coevolution Quarterly. Point Foundation, Box 428, Sausalito, California 94965 $12/year

Footnotes to the Future. Futuremics, Inc. 2850 Connecticut Ave., N.W., Washington, D.C. 20006 Monthly $15/year

Futures. IPC Science and Technology Press Ltd., IPC House, 32 High St., Guilford, Surrey, England. Bimonthly $65/year

The Futurist. World Future Society, 4916 St. Elmo Ave., (Bethesda), Washington, D.C. 20014 Bimonthly $15/year

Working Papers for a New Society. 123 Mount Auburn Street, Cambridge, Mass. 02138 Quarterly, $10/year

World Future Society Bulletin. World Future Society. Bimonthly.

Additional information concerning individuals and organizations can be found in *The Future: A Guide to Information Sources* (Washington, D.C.: The World Future Society, 1977).

Appendix

Guidelines for the Determination of Objectives for Futures Education Programs

1.0 *Futures education should attempt to help students understand the concept of alternative futures.*

1.1 Students should be given opportunities to investigate a variety of alternative futures.

1.2 Students should be given opportunities to understand the differences among possible, probable, and preferable futures.

2.0 *Futures education should aid the student to understand the concept of change.*

2.1 Students should be aided to understand the various ways of anticipating, coping with, and adapting to change.

2.2 Students should be aided to understand the possible effects of changes on their personal goals and aspirations.

3.0 *Futures education should promote an understanding of the possible modifications in human behavior necessary for the future.*

3.1 Students should be aided to understand and appreciate the need for wider and more active involvement in public affairs.

3.2 Students should be aided to understand the need for more cooperative and socially responsible behavior in the future.

3.3 Students should be aided to understand the ways in which ordinary individuals can influence the course of future developments.

3.4 Students should be encouraged to become more creative and imaginative in dealing with future possibilities.

4.0 *Futures education should promote a holistic view of the natural and social worlds.*

4.1 Students should be aided to understand the concept of "spaceship earth" and the effects of human activities on the ecological system.

4.2 Students should be aided to understand the concept of human interdependence in a global society.

4.3 Students should be aided to understand the interdependencies of interacting "systems" such as the ecological system, the economic system, nation-state system, etc.

5.0 *Futures education should promote an understanding of important societal trends and their implications.*

5.1 Students should be aided to understand the major dilemmas facing the world from such trends as population growth, pollution, energy shortages, etc.

5.2 Students should be aided to understand dilemmas presented by trends in a variety of areas such as technology, biomedical research, international relations, work and leisure, computer science, communications, etc.

5.3 Students should be provided with opportunities to investigate alternative approaches to these dilemmas.

6.0 *Futures education should promote an understanding of the relationships between values and the future.*

6.1 Students should be aided to understand the nature of values, their effects on human behavior, and their social, economic, political, and environmental consequences.

6.2 Students should be given opportunities to clarify and consider the implications of their own values with respect to the future.

Continued on next page

7.0 *Futures education should promote an understanding of the ideas of major futurists and the methods of futurism.*

7.1 Students should be aided to become familiar with the important contributions to futurist thought and how these can be applied to the study of contemporary issues.

7.2 Students should be given opportunities to develop skill at using a variety of forecasting methodologies.

8.0 *Futures education should promote an understanding of the relationships between past, present, and future.*

8.1 Students should be aided to understand that the future begins in the present and that actions taken today will help to determine the shape of things to come.

8.2 Students should, while studying the future, be encouraged to maintain an appreciation for the past and for those ideas and values which have lasting significance.

9.0 *Futures education should promote a variety of additional perspectives and inquiry strategies.*

9.1 Students should be given opportunities to develop images of alternative futures.

9.2 Students should be encouraged to use a variety of inductive, deductive, intuitive, and creative thinking strategies to investigate and contemplate the future.

9.3 Students should be given opportunities to develop and express their own personal goals and aspirations for the future.

9.4 Students should be encouraged to maintain an optimistic attitude toward the future, despite the serious dilemmas which the world faces.

10.0 *Futures education should promote the general improvement of basic research and communications skills.*

10.1 Students should be given opportunities to read challenging materials and to locate information in a wide variety of ways.

10.2 Students should be given opportunities to communicate their feelings, attitudes, and ideas about the future in ways which demonstrate their competencies in written and oral expression.

Index

Index prepared by Mary Monk
Book design and production by Joseph Perez
Cover design by Bill Caldwell
Typography by Byrd PrePress
Printing and binding by Waverly Press